ESSENTIALS OF MEDITATION

Robert Maitland

ESSENTIALS
OF
MEDITATION

by
Robert Maitland

csa press
lakemont, georgia
30552

Copyright © 1975
by Robert Maitland

Standard Book Number 0-87707-157-8

Library of Congress Catalog Number 75-11136

Printed in the United States of America
by CSA Printing and Bindery, Inc.

This book is dedicated to Korean Zen Master Il Bung Seo, Kyung Bo, a man who knows where all men come from.

Korean Zen Master
Il Bung Seo Kyung Bo

CONTENTS

FOREWORD	11
MEDITATION	13
BEGINNING	17
CONDITIONING	21
RELAXATION	31
INNER EXPLORATION	39
THE CENTERS	45
TIME AND PLACE	51
THE SEAT	55
THE ATTITUDE	65
DEALING WITH DISTRACTIONS	67
MEDITATION ON BREATH WITH COUNTING	71
MEDITATION ON BREATH	75
MEDITATION ON BREATH IN THE NOSTRILS	79
MEDITATION ON RISE AND FALL	83
MEDITATION ON BREATH IN THE TANJUN	87
A BREATHING CYCLE	93
WALKING MEDITATION	97
THE CONFRONTATION	99
MEDITATION ON THOUGHTS	105
A MEDITATION	115
CHIGWAN TAJA MEDITATION	119
MEDITATION IN DAILY LIFE	125
ODDS, ENDS AND OPINIONS	129
ABOUT THE AUTHOR	137

Foreword

It has been said that there are two basic paths to Realization: that of expansion, which opens to include all phenomena, and that of contraction, which reduces to the very center of the source of Being. In Western tradition these have been called the "positive" and "negative" ways or the "centrifugal" or "centripetal" paths. In this comprehensive and sincere book by the Rev. Tae-Chi Maitland many alternatives are shown. The examples drawn from Yoga are taken from the former approach while those from the Zen tradition illustrate the latter.

Ultimate Reality is undivided and indescribable. The last word dissolves in silence. The light of understanding leaves no trace of the ghost of self. By the motiveless action of the Unborn, all is accomplished.

Meditation halts the frantic egocentric activity and illusory thinking expressive of desire and grasping based on ignorance. Resistance to the given conjures up "one who resists." Released from spasm, "the fluteplayer plays as he will." Amnesia gone, the king wakes in his own chair. The flower is red; the willow is green.

Ven. Song-Ryong Hearn.
Zen Master.

1

MEDITATION

Meditation is an activity quite strange to Western society. It is no part of our religious heritage as Christians. We have heard of "contemplative" monks among the mystics but their techniques were quite different from the meditative practices of the oriental religions. Meditation has reached the west in the last twenty years or so, springing from Japanese and Korean Zen and Indian Yoga sects primarily. It has been received with both joy and suspicion; with joy by those who interpret it as a path to self-knowledge, psychotherapy or God-knowledge, and with suspicion by those who consider it a threat to their religion or as a dropout mechanism for those no longer willing to produce and consume.

It is not difficult to examine western society and decry its competitive, grasping nature; its pretenses, inequities, injustices and debatable values. But, that same society is producing a spiritual energy, spiritual hunger and a longing for freedom of the soul in all classes of society and in all walks of life.

"Reality" is said to be always in harmony, in a delicate balance which is perfect just as it is, regardless of how we choose to interpret it. And so society produces the need for meditation in our lives.

All religions have their devotional sects—Christian, Buddhist, Moslem, Hindu. These by their very nature tend to separate man and God. Even the most devoted is praying to something else in whose existence "he" believes. But oriental religions basically say otherwise, contrary to our traditional western religious beliefs. Zen, Advaita Vedanta, Taoism and essential Sufism hold that there is no separate God, as such, and that ultimate reality is a unity; pure, complete, perfect unity. Hence the goal is to achieve union with or rather union in, this ultimate unity. All plurality is illusory. There are not two worlds, the illusory and the real: We are that ultimate reality. Christianity declares the path to God by love through prayer. Buddhism declares the path to Original Nature by self-effort through meditation. The one is a matter of belief, the other a matter of experiment.

It would be a good thing for each of us to take time to investigate the nature of belief, for our own benefit, to see it as it is, to ask "What do I really do when I believe?"

The message from the Orient says that there is a way out of this transitory existence; that it can be done and anyone can do it but the path is hard and there is no magical way of making it easy. No one can walk that path for us, neither God nor man. We must tread for ourselves. The prospect of such an effort is not a happy one for some but for others it will be like returning home.

Meditation then is an experiment to be performed, to be conducted through psychological introspection. All experi-

Meditation

ments require basic assumptions before they can be designed. Let's take for example an experiment involving light in order to study its nature. First we assume that light comes in bundles of energy with mass like bullets. If this is so, then we should be able to intercept a beam of light and measure the force on an inserted plate due to the change in momentum of the intercepted light particles and so verify the assumptions.

The meditation experiment assumes that man's original nature is "unity" and that it can be known as a fact in this life. The experiment takes on many designs. Generally there is the Zen way, the Theravadin way, the Yoga way, the Sufi way, the way of the Christian Mystic and perhaps no way at all. Ultimately each way is unique. Your way will be your own. For example, there is Burroughs Zen, Cleveland Zen, Bishop Zen, Englebert Zen, etc. The personal path seems to be made in this instant to be trod in the next. For a path to exist first one must take a step, then another and yet another . . . .

It is no easy task if carried to the end. It is said that in order to see into his own nature man must transform his very self and relinquish that which he prizes most. Although many benefits accrue from the practice of meditation, the aim of meditation is crystal clear; it is self-realization and nothing less is acceptable.

There are some who believe that no matter how conceived, if existing in any fashion whatsoever, God has no prejudices, holds no grudges but makes Himself available to every man, in every moment, in every way possible. His grace is given freely to the pure and impure alike. There is no one from whom God excludes Himself.

The problem is with man. We simply do not see correctly. There is something wrong with the manner in which we view reality. We cannot see "God," our "Original Nature" because we perceive in error. We must overcome this somehow, so that we can perceive directly, the "Suchness" which we are. We must transcend ordinary awareness, experience, thought and perception and intuitively realize the nature of mind by a spontaneous leap of supra-rational insight. Meditation sets man's transformation process into motion.

Part of the problem is that we have involved ourselves and allowed ourselves to be conditioned by the flow of outside circumstances and now consider ourselves to be static, separate entities rather than part of the ebb and flow of a formative, transitory process and **we must see this.** It is a matter of digging deeper, below the strata of conceptual personality, built up in the course of time in the process of becoming, a matter of **remembering** our Original Nature.

Perhaps all is well. Perhaps there are no "wrong" paths. Perhaps each path is perfect and contains "not one speck of dust". Regardless of our religious convictions let us start the experiment, the trek to "Suchness." Perhaps the Christ, the Buddha, Lao Tzu, the progenitors of the religions of man **shared a common experience.** Perhaps their qualifications for Realization were little better than our own. If it was possible for them, it is also possible for us. So let's begin now and make the most sustained effort of which we are capable.

2

BEGINNING

It is not so easy to get started in meditation. Meditation training is available but it is highly localized in the USA mostly to be found on the west coast and the northeast sections. Enlightened teachers are rare indeed but that really doesn't matter. There is much that one can do for oneself prior to meeting his teacher. It is said that there are more good teachers than good disciples. A Zen Master will tell you that to learn Zen three things are needed: A Zen Master a Zen Temple and friends. We may have to begin with nothing but friends.

Much literature is available on meditation and a perusal thereof quickly convinces us that the beneficial influences of meditation are both desirable and valid. Who for example does not desire better mental health and stability, relief from tension, calmness and objectivity? But after much reading one will still not meditate. Many texts say too much about meditation and too little concerning how to meditate. Good material exists in all books but it takes experience to sort it out. Some texts such as Theravadin Buddhist Meditations are very highly systematized and swamp the would-be student to the point that he doesn't know where to begin. Many meditations are simply too difficult for the beginner to execute. Many meditational texts are devoted to a particular sect with overemphasis on a particular way with the implication that it is the sole way, the highest way, the ancient way, the kings way or the Buddhas way. This tends to turn off those of us who have just managed to free ourselves from an "only" way. Many texts are compilations of classic texts and the author is obviously a scholar not a meditator. Sect oriented manuals are often written by loving devotees expounding the master's teachings which are highly compacted and difficult to understand.

What's most disconcerting is that we don't comprehend what we read. The language of meditation is to a degree, a technical language and must be assimilated as direct inner experience. Without some inner orientation, we cannot execute the admonitions of the text. For example, one is advised to search within and find the place of silence, to expand the circle of silence and guard its periphery in daily life. This is not impossible but must seem so to the beginner.

Another difficulty is that we have this conditioned way of learning in which we tend to read and store conceptual information for later recall to pass tests or to manipulate as symbols in problem solving. In connection with meditation we must learn to relate what we read to our own experience **as we read.** This implies we must do some meditating before we read too much and must alternate reading with practice. Oh my friend, so very much depends upon persistent effort over a long period of time. As a sage once said, "Enlightenment is not difficult to achieve. Only two things are ncessary. One need only begin and then continue."

No "put down" has been intended in criticism of meditation books. Each one is perfect. As you read and re-read during the course of the evolution of your meditation practice you will learn exactly what is necessary for you at that time. As experience in meditation accumulates, inner references develop which make such subjects as energy, stilling the mind, objective watchfulness, choiceless awareness and so forth meaningful reality.

In the Orient, as a result of cultural background, students naturally place complete faith in Guru. Americans on the other hand are more often competitive, goal oriented strivers who need to understand what they are doing and why. In the chapters which follow an attempt is made to satisfy this requirement and it proceeds in the following way. Get in shape and stay in shape. Learn to relax and direct awareness within, to those places where the action is. Get familiar with the energy centers and get control of the energy. Learn to "set up" for meditation regarding time, place, position and attitude. Master a sequence of meditations, increasing in difficulty through a succession of breath exercises to the more difficult meditations on thoughts and total awareness. Learn to deal with yourself in confrontation with your own predicament. Then when your teacher appears you will be ready for him. Assume the responsibility **now** for your own spiritual progress. To begin, read Chapter Three and practice, practice, practice. And know that there are those who are sincerely concerned with your development and truly wish you spiritual success along your way.

3

CONDITIONING

If you visit a Zen training temple you will notice that the students in training generally have a free hour from five to six o'clock just prior to dinner. They will not be resting; they will be exercising. By this time they will have arisen at four a.m., meditated for four hours, eaten twice, performed kitchen chores and housekeeping, worked about four and one half hours on Temple maintenance and the winter wood supply in addition to attending school. One would think they had exercised enough. True—but wrong kind. The meditator needs flexibility and durability of body, and Yoga postures supply that. Additionally when practiced prior to meditation the muscles relax, protest less and are quieter. Thus, conditioning is required. Flexibility is necessary for a good seat. The older the meditator the more vital becomes regular conditioning. Yoga postures loosen the joints, stretch the vertabrae, tone the nervous system, the musculature and enhance awareness. Hatha Yoga, as a practice, has grown rapidly in the West, and teachers and Ashrams abound where it is used. Good books are readily available if you are especially interested. We have found that meditation goes better if one exercises first. If one meditates first he will probably exercise second.

The purpose here then, is conditioning as a prerequisite to meditation, and a working, practical system is presented, primarily for the readers convenience. One can add, delete, or modify the exercises to suit the individual—and one should.

The exercises and postures will be presented in the sequence in which they should be executed simply because they save time and flow together readily. The flow is important, the rhythm is helpful.

A few suggestions may assist:
- Once started don't make any sudden moves.
- Always move mindfully and deliberately.
- Keep the attention on the muscles under stress; that is, those in tension.
- Maintain position until the muscles are extended.
- Pain will be present at first and is simply a sign that muscles are stretching. One can regulate the pain by holding an attitude until the pain recedes then forcing the posture until pain appears, then holding until it recedes.
- Better yet, relax into position.
- Rather than hurry to finish, try to maintain a continuous awareness of body throughout the practice period and work methodically.
- Normally each yogic posture has a corresponding breathing sequence. They generally occur quite naturally as the posture compresses or allows the lungs to expand. If one finds the breathing troublesome look up the posture in an appropriate text.

Conditioning 23

Postures are done alone or in a group. The main advantage of group exercise is regularity. Additionally, people support each other's effort. The sequence of exercises which follow are illustrated for your convenience.

Having found an appropriate place, stand quietly arms at the sides and follow the natural flow of breath. Do not regulate it in any way. Count each exhalation from one to ten then repeat. Do so three times. Set the attention so as to watch yourself perform the exercises.

The Vertical Stretch

Raise the arms overhead, place the feet together and stretch toward the ceiling.

Half Moon

Clasp the hands together, bend the body into a bow first right then left holding the position a few moments while the muscles of the side stretch. Repeat until you feel as though the muscles are extended.

Head Rotation

Lower the hands to the sides and rotate the head first in one direction then the other. Start in small circles and then go to larger ones. Do nothing rapidly. After a little practice you will dwell in certain positions to extend the large neck and other related muscles. One is surprised at the noise induced as the cervicals are flexed.

Shoulder Roll

Standing erect, hands on hips simultaneously roll the shoulders forward in circles extending the muscles as far as possible, work at moderate speeds. Reverse the process, rolling them in the opposite sense. One feels them loosen and relax.

Hip Swing

Place the hands on the buttocks, palms just under the waistline with the feet placed about six inches apart. Arch forward keeping shoulders and head above the feet to maintain balance and swing the hips in a circle to the left. Make the circle small at first then increase the diameter. One feels the vertabrae riffle like a card deck from the base of the spine up the column of the vertabrae. After some half dozen rotations reverse the direction.

Backbend

With the hands still on the buttocks bend backward, arching the body, stretching the anterior muscles of the body. Return to the vertical and arch again. About three repetitions are sufficient.

Standing Head to Knee

Standing erect, bend over slowly as far as you can with the breath exhaled. Simply touch the hands to the floor or grasp the ankles as the body relaxes and the back and leg muscles extend. A few repetitions will do.

Seated Position

Assume the seated position, trunk erect, head erect, legs extended together, arms straight, hand on knees. Collect yourself, breath regularly and watch the breath.

Posterior Stretch

Exhale a bit, bend forward, relax and stretch but don't pull the body forward. Keep the legs straight, knees unbent. Grasp the big toe of each foot and lower the elbows to the ground outside the knees. The body and head lie against the upper part of the legs. This is difficult to do. If the toes cannot be reached, grasp the ankles or knees. Relax as consciously as possible.

Extended Leg Pull

This posture is assumed both left and right. Assume the seated position, spread the legs and tuck the heel of the right leg into the crotch with the foot parallel to the left thigh. Bend toward the outstretched leg and grasp the sole of the foot with the left hand. Bend the body toward the leg, head to knee. If the foot cannot be reached use the ankle. Place the right hand on the toes and continue to relax into position. It is most important to proceed slowly. The muscles extended form a circle from the left heel, along the calves, the hamstrings of the leg, across the buttocks, up the right side and along the right arm. Proceed cautiously and don't strain. The exercise is then repeated with the right leg extended.

Head to Toe

Draw the heels toward the crotch and place the soles of the feet together. Cup the hands around the feet with the elbows outside the legs and relax the forehead to the toes. Thereafter, assume the corpse position.

Corpse

The corpse position is much used, particularly during relaxation exercises. One lies flat on the back, neck flat on the floor. No pillow is used. Place the legs and feet together and let the feet fall outward, hands outward, palms up.

Plough

From the corpse position, raise the legs slowly keeping them straight until they are vertical. Continue to bring the legs over the head until they are parallel to the ground then lower the toes to the ground as close to the head as possible. As the feet are placed farther and farther above the head, tension mounts in the spine.

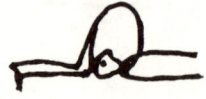

Extended Plough

From the plough position simply lower the knees around the head and clasp the ears with them. Thereafter, return to the plough position.

Conditioning

Shoulder Stand

Place the hands on the back for support and from the hips elevate the legs to the vertical. Use the supporting hands as little as possible. The trunk and legs are vertical, the weight on the shoulders and neck, the chin against the chest.

Shoulder Bridge

From the shoulder stand split the legs in a scissors fashion bending the knees to maintain balance. Supporting the back with the hands and arching the back, lower the feet to the floor while supporting the body weight on the shoulders and the back of the neck. Grasp the ankles with the hands and stretch the back into an arch.

Wheel

From the bridge position place the hands above the shoulders and press the body upward arching the back as much as possible. To withdraw from the position, lower the head to the floor, roll down the neck to the shoulders, relax the arch and collapse the legs. Return to the corpse position, roll over and lie face down.

Cobra

Place the palms against the ground just above the level of the shoulders. Slowly, continuously raise the head until the shoulders lift. Continue as far as possible. Then using the arms, continue to arch as far as possible without raising the waist from the ground.

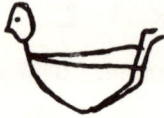

Bow

Face downward, bend the legs at the knees. Reach back and grasp the ankles. Use the legs to draw the ankles away from the body and the knees off the ground until the weight of the body rests on the abdomen. Slowly return to the prone position.

At first the sequence will require some 30 minutes for a good workout. With practice, 20 minutes will do. Be deliberate, continually aware and ignore the efforts of others. You are not competing.

Do not be discouraged if difficulty is encountered with the execution, as time goes on one becomes remarkably flexible.

4

RELAXATION

Our society, reflecting our own natures, competitive, violent and grasping, indeed induces pressures and tensions which must be alleviated. The resulting emotional and mental stresses can be relieved through deliberate relaxation. There are many methods and they all work if sufficiently practiced. The relaxation method presented here is one which can be applied as a group or an individual technique. It is not implied that a relaxation method is a prerequisite to meditation. Such is not the case. But something must be done at day's end to reduce the tension and the internal excitement (noise) if we are to perceive internal activity, especially if we have not had much experience in meditation.

The relaxation method described here is used to quiet body-mind thru the process of muscular relaxation and the use of breath. The attention of meditators is first directed within to develop awareness and concentration and then expanded to encompass total awareness—inside and outside.

This relaxation method is best performed as a group

activity at first with an instructor calling directions. The reason is that the process of remembering the suggestions, the actions and the instruction sequence gets in the way of the relaxation itself. Nevertheless if an individual practices with persistence the process becomes automatic and relaxation follows quickly.

One of the main difficulties with teaching meditation is the matter of language. Science, in a very orderly manner has divided external reality, a single continuum, into parts and assigned labels and qualities thereto. These can be pointed to and thus have a level of reality. The inner world, the non-physical, the mental world has received less attention. The division and labeling of the mental life and internal phenomena such as emotions and states of mind has not received the same level of division. Furthermore one has little confidence in classic concepts of the inner man since the labels so often are not in one to one correspondence with anything to be found inside. For example, find the conscious mind, subliminual consciousness, the mind, the superego. Most important of all, find the ego.

The upshot of all this is, that to know yourself, you must look for yourself, and that knowing will not require words. But we must start somewhere and we will develop what language we need as we go.

Feel yourself breathe! Do it now! Really feel the breath. Something knows it is breathing. Something feels, senses, the breath. Now watch that something that watches the breath.

Repeat your name to yourself! Do you hear the sound of your name in your head? Something hears the sound. Now watch that something that hears your name.

Relaxation

Look at the book in your hands! Something sees the book. Feel the something seeing the book. Now watch that something that sees the book. Feel that something to the exclusion of all else. The Indians call that something "the witness" and so shall we. That is probably what you really mean when you say "I." Mark it well! One sees much of it during meditation. That witness is a point of awareness and you know that it can be present. As a matter of fact when it is present you are aware, when it is not you are distracted or asleep though awake.

The witness feels the breath, hears the name, sees the book. The witness is the subject. The breath, the name, and the book are objects of meditation. The attention was directed to each object of meditation in turn. Do so now! Redirect attention to each object of meditation in turn the breath, the name and the book but only while the "witness" is present.

Lets "look" at a few more objects of meditation. Arouse the witness. Know you are present. Focus the attention on, direct awareness to, look at the heartbeat. Feel exclusively, as intensely as possible the beating heart and know you are feeling it. The "witness" is present. The heartbeat is present.

Arouse the witness, that is, know you are feeling, and direct attention to the muscles of the face. Feel the muscles of the face exclusively. "Watch" them. Now fixate on the muscles around the eyes, around the mouth, inside the mouth. Fixate on the breath! Resume reading. Watch the witness from time to time during the day.

The relaxation scenario which follows is presented for an instructor performing guided, group relaxation. If an individual wishes to auto-relax it is not difficult to modify the proceedure to one of self suggestion.

The principle of all relaxation methods consist of four functions; fixation, suggestion, pause, and sensation. The object is to eliminate tension by relaxing the muscles of the body just as if the body is preparing for sleep. The system used here uses the breath as a pausing mechanism to give the suggestion time to work as well as to provide a functional suggestion. The student fixates, the instructor suggests, the student pauses by counting down the breath and then sensates.

The corpse position is assumed by the student lying on a mat or rug, nothing too soft. The instructor begins.

Fix the attention on the breath, the whole breath body. Arouse the witness, know you are watching the breath. Cyclically count the exhalations only; breath three, breath two, breath one, breath zero. Repeat five times.

Fixate, focus attention on the scalp, feel the condition of the scalp exclusively. The muscles of the scalp are relaxing, with each breath they are relaxing more and more. Pause and count down the breath exhalations, breaths three, two, one, zero. Feel the muscles of the scalp relaxing. Be aware of the witness. The attention is on the scalp.

Deliberately, smoothly redirect attention to, fixate on, the face. The muscles of the forehead are relaxing. Feel them. The muscles of the cheeks are relaxing, the muscles of the mouth, around the mouth, inside the mouth are relaxing. Fix the attention on all the muscles of the face. The muscles of the face are relaxing; with each breath they are relaxing more and more. Countdown the breath three, two, one, zero. The entire face is drooping slightly, the face is calm. Feel the muscles of the face relax.

Relaxation

Mindfully shift the attention to the neck, sense the heavy muscles on the sides of the neck, feel deep inside the neck. The muscles of the neck are relaxing more and more with each gentle breath. Countdown the breath. Feel the muscles relax.

The mind is clear. The mind is alert. The mind is not drowsy, not sleepy. The mind is cool, aware and indifferent.

Direct the attention to the muscles of the back. Start with the large muscles in the back of the neck. Let the attention flow thru the heavy muscles high on the back and down the spine into the small of the back. Fix all the muscles of the back in the awareness. Work hard! The muscles of the back are relaxing with each gentle easy breath. With the attention fixed in the back muscles countdown the breath, three, two, one, and zero. Sense the relaxation taking place.

Relaxation is flowing up around the rib cage, along the dorsal muscles and into the shoulders, across the shoulders and into the arms. Focus the attention in the arms, both arms, upper arms and fore-arms. The arms are relaxing with each breath. Down count the breath. The attention is in the forearms. Feel them relax.

Fix the attention on the muscles of the chest. The muscles of the chest are relaxing, relaxing. Count down the breath. Feel the muscles of the chest relax.

Direct the attention to abdominals. The muscles of the abdominals are relaxing, with each breath they are relaxing more and more. Pause, count down the breath and feel the abdominals relax.

Relaxation now, is spreading to the entire chest cavity.

Fix the attention in the chest cavity. It is quieting, relaxing with each gentle, easy breath. Down count the breath. Feel all the organs in the chest cavity relaxing.

The entire upper body is relaxed now; the mind is awake, alert, clear and calm. Relaxation flows easily in the body. Fix the attention on the belly below the navel, above the pelvis, deep through the belly, and the sex organs. Hold on! Fixate. The belly, its interior is relaxing with each breath. Down count the breath; three, two, one, zero.

Fixate on the buttocks and the muscles of the hips. They are relaxing, relaxing as you watch. Shift the attention to the heavy muscles of the thighs watch closely! Down count. Now add the muscles of the thighs, lower legs, the calves. Feel your way along the inside. And while holding the awareness of thighs and calves, add the feet. The muscles of the legs are relaxing, with each breath they are relaxing more and more. Hold attention in the legs. Count down the breath and feel the legs relax.

The entire body is relaxed now, the mind quiet and alert, emotions subdued, tensions gone, the body clean and pure. All is safe and secure. Run the attention thru the body from head to toe and back. Proceed at your own discretion. Be complete, methodical and thorough.

Now fix the entire body in the awareness. Work hard. Do not strain but try to feel it all at once. The entire body is relaxing with each breath. Countdown the breath, three, two, one, and zero.

Feel the entire body relaxing. Now fix the attention on the breath, simply follow the natural flow of breath.

When the exercise is finished arouse yourself as if from

Relaxation

sleep. Take time, move easily and take any comfortable, seated position.

The relaxation scenario is lengthy, repetitious and somewhat boring but it has advantages. First it can be read directly to students by an instructor until its pattern emerges and he can modify it to advantage. Secondly the individual student can tape it, carefully insert pauses for breath counting and by play back use it on himself. If one does so, suggestion becomes unnecessary as time goes by and ultimately relaxation ensures simply by fixating on the muscle groups and repetitiously downcounting the breath. It can be done almost any time or place and of itself has real value when applied in daily life.

It is necessary to alert the mind from time to time during its use. This is fairly easily accomplished as the mind becomes more suggestable as the exercise proceeds. When classes are held in the evening for meditation the method inevitably puts students to sleep at first. This is to be expected since the position, the relaxation, the shallow breathing are all normal prerequisites to the sleeping condition.

The primary purpose of the exercise, however, where used with meditation training is fourfold; first to subdue the body functions, second, to slow down the mental activity, third, to provide "witness" training and finally to learn to direct attention within.

It is important because in the relaxed state one can more easily explore his inner condition and get some training in doing so. Meditation involves everything happening both within and without—not just thoughts. And now that the body is in a condition to be surveyed perhaps it would be helpful to know what to look for and how to train for meditation.

5

INNER EXPLORATION

Inner exploration is the art of directed inner awareness, a way of looking within to determine the state of your being, the state of your relative reality. What is observed within and without is that and nothing else. It is where we are and no place else. The point of Western man's ignorance of his internal makeup is not to be belaboured but chances are excellent that few of us have looked within or if so, only cursorily.

The practice again may be performed with an instructor calling directions or by the student directing himself.

For beginners in meditation a good time to practice inner awareness is immediately following the relaxation exercise. However it is important to arouse oneself, change positions and stretch before resuming the corpse position and beginning inner exploration. It is advisable to remain aware of the breath during the interlude so as to remain centered. The body-mind will remain calm.

Attitude during the exercise is important simply because cerebration should be minimal. Thinking should not be supressed. Rather it should be ignored and not encouraged. An attitude of detached indifference, a cool, quiet awareness should be maintained, the Witness ever present. If some startling discovery is made, don't intellectualize. Don't conceptualize. For example, "Fear is found in the Solar Plexus." Simply know it. Internal division of self into functional concepts is only a matter of expedience for self knowledge. Let the scholars do it. Let us know by a simple wordless knowing. I repeat: Let us try not to intellectualize internal phenomena. It will only cause difficulty later. Rather let us recognize events through "pattern recognition," the recognition of process. When conceptualization manifests—then *move on*.

That is not to say that internal conceptualization has no value. Without it one can not communicate with other meditators. But intellectualize after inner exploration, in retrospect. Post process data; no real time, on-line processing.

We shall explore essentially four categories of being: internal body volumes, the chakras or plexuses, the six senses (includes mind), and the faculty of speech.

In many meditation texts one is enjoined to "look at" the mind, the emotions, the bodily sensations. It means arouse the Witness. Then focus attention on the object and feel it exclusively, ignoring other phenomena. It will be used here. Indeed the directed feeling around within ourselves feels like a looking or seeing process as the practitioner will soon discover.

Assume the corpse position, fixate on the breath and let body-mind relax.

Inner Exploration

Look at the following body volumes, calmly and directly. By all means be deliberate and redirect attention with continuity. Slide, shift, flow from object to object:

- The whole head
- The neck
- The shoulders
- The arms
- The chest
- The whole abdominal cavity
- The rise and fall of the abdomen
- The heartbeat
- The belly
- The sexual organs
- The hips
- The buttocks
- The upper legs
- The lower legs
- The feet
- The entire body

Focus the attention more precisely and poke around inside. Seek out the nooks and crannies. Go "where the action is." Fix the attention on the breath, the whole breath. Center and collect yourself. Know that the Witness watches the breath. Pause for a while . . . .

Direct the attention to the centers. A prolonged looking is necessary. They are the points in the body where most "feelings" seem to originate. This, one must see for oneself.

- Focus the attention in the cerebral center in the top of the skull. Activity here is slight except when rather severe tension is present or a persistent headache exists. It seems to have the effect of intensifying the feeling of the Witness.
- Fix the attention on the throat center located in the lower front of the neck.
- Fix the attention on the heart center located in the center of the chest and middle of the body near the heartbeat. Persistent attention to this center will elicit a response which must be personally felt to be identified. It is generally quiet but is very active if a stimulant such as coffee or tea has been taken excessively or when waking up from a bad dream.
- Fix the attention on the solar plexus, a large nerve gangion centered about two inches below the sternum. This center is generally quite active except when calm. It responds when tension, anger, hate and fear are present, and its characteristic sensation or feeling is easily identified. A prolonged awareness of this center during the emotional crisis of daily life can teach one much about oneself.
- Fix the attention on the navel center located about three inches below the navel and three inches in the body. The response however, seems to come from the front just inside the belly. This center seems to be associated with the vital energy of the body and is most active when one is excited, keyed up, or sexually aroused.
- Fix the attention on the base center located about three inches above the anus behind the pelvis. This center is aroused during sexual excitement and also responds to prolonged attention.

The navel and base centers seem to interact sympathetically, when one is active so is the other.

Inner Exploration

Generally speaking, during meditation, the solar and navel centers are those primarily involved. Focus the attention on the breath. Pause for a while—.
Direct attention to the senses. One repeats again and again, ad infinitum, ad nauseam, keep the Witness present, the senser alive. Know you are feeling. Be **mindful.**

- Fixate on the tongue and mouth. Use a small piece of candy. Taste intensely!
- Fixate on pressure points of the body on the floor. Feel intensely!
- Open the eyes. Watch intensely all within the range of vision. Know that you are seeing!
- Fix the attention on external sounds. Welcome all noises into awareness. Listen with care.
- Fix the attention in the nostrils. Smell all odors, the body perspiration, the incense.
- Look back in the mind where the thoughts are. Try to see them start and stop. Do not interfere. Do not support the thoughts. Do not become involved, merely observe. From what point do thoughts arise? What kinds of thoughts exist within? Are thoughts heard, seen or felt?
- Recite a poem to yourself. Little boy blue come blow your horn . . . Know you are speaking. How do you know what to say when you speak?

Inner awareness can be practiced at any time, in any position, under any circumstances. The procedure is simple and orderly; concentrate on significant body volumes from head to toe, plexuses from top to bottom, the senses and the speaking function. Much of the day comprises speaking and listening. Be mindful during these activities.

When one practices thus, one sees the emotional patterns, the thought patterns. The sensed condition is one's own phenomenal reality.

6

THE CENTERS

It is advisable to know something of the chakras or centers of psychic energy that exist within. The centers were first defined thousands of years ago in Indian Yogic literature. Whether defined or not you would learn of them during the course of the practice of meditation. It is a fact that energy in the body flows with the attention and tends to accumulate in natural storage locations in the body. They can be discovered also because they respond to emotion; energy in the belly, fear in the solar plexus, love in the cardiac plexus, tension in the command plexus and so forth. Sometimes spontaneously, energy moves among the centers and vibration, heat, shaking or perspiration occurs. The chakras, whatever they are, are perceptible and will sooner or later be experienced directly by the meditator.

According to Yogic philosophy, a vital energy called prana is found in all forms of life. It is not thought of as consciousness or spirit but is an energy used by atman, individual soul, in its material and astral manifestations. It is thought to permeate all matter and controls and regulates the very cells comprising the body. It is that which animates matter.

Prana is absorbed by humans through the food, water and the air they consume. The finest manifestation of prana action is thought; the grossest, the motion of the lungs. Pranic energy can be acquired, stored and controlled by breathing exercises called "pranayama."

Pranayama extracts prana from the air and stores it in various nerve centers. The main storage centers are in the solar plexus, the hypogastric plexus (naval center) and the brain. Pranayama then, energizes and controls the flow of energy throughout the human nervous system.

This implies an "energy body," or an astral body, or an etheric body, which exists in coincidence with the physical body wherein the chakras, or energy centers of yogic lore, are in juxtaposition with the mass nerve centers, ganglia, or plexuses of the human nervous system. The chakra, location, corresponding plexus and common name are delineated in the following paragraphs:

The Muladhara chakra is located at the base of the spine near the cocyx and above the anus. Here located is the pelvic plexus with branches to the root of the penis. It is also called the base center or earth center.

The Swadisthana chakra is located a fingers length below the naval in the center of the body, directly above the earth center. Here is located the hypogastric plexus. It is also called the naval center and the lower tanjun.

The Manipura chakra centers a finger length below the sternum in the middle front of the body. Here is located the solar plexus. It is also called the solar center and the middle tanjun.

The Centers

The Anahata chakra is located in the region of the heart. Here is located the cardiac plexus. It is also called the heart center.

The Visudha chakra is located in the front of the throat and is called the throat center. Here is located the Pharyngeal plexus.

The Agna chakra is located at a point between the eyebrows and is called the third eye. Here is located the Nasociliary plexus and/or the command plexus.

The Sahasrara chakra is located in the brain in the crown of the head. It is called the Brahma chakra, the cerebral center and the upper tanjun. Its corresponding plexus is the brain.

The description of the Chakras and their connections (all connected serially from bottom to top in the order delineated) runs parallel with the description of the Right Vagus nerve and its connections with the sympathetic plexuses. The plexuses of the sympathetic nervous system have sensory and motor communication branches with the posterior nerve roots of the spinal cord which are connected by centripetal fibers to the brain.

It is interesting to note that the Right Vagus nerve is more plentifully supplied with afferent and efferent fibers than the Left and gains direct connection with the solar plexus and the pelvic plexus thru the hypogastric plexus or lower tanjun. The stimulation of the Right Vagus nerve can thus control the activities of, or energize all the six plexuses of the sympathetic nervous system.

This seems consistent with Taoist tradition which states that Chi energy, the vital energy, is stored in the lower tanjun, or naval center, and is from there distributed to the remainder of the body as required.

Kundalini energy is stored in the Muhladhara chakra at the base of the spine. It is defined as the creative impetus from the Divine, the individual prana, the center of residual sensations, the static anabolic and katabolic power of the sympathetic nervous system, and the coiled up energy of action. Take your choice but do not believe the kundalini energy does not exist in the muhladhara chakra or earth center.

There are ten subtle paths thru which nerve currents flow, according to Yoga, and three are of major importance: the ida, pingala, and sushumna. The sushumna corresponds to the hollow central canal of the spine, the ida to the bundle of efferent, sensory fibers and the pingala to the afferent, motor fibers in the spinal cord along which nerve impulses are conveyed. The Yogi, by practices of pranayama, breath control, mudras which are postures to excite the flow of nerve currents, bandhas which are locks or postures involving muscular contraction to control the flow of energy in the sushumna, and meditation on chakras, activates the sushumna.

Ordinarily the sushumna at the base of which the kundalini resides in the muhladhara is closed, but when the canal is opened (and the yogi makes every effort to open it), prana acts upon the coiled power of kundalini. It then enters the sushumna nerve conduit and is consciously caused to travel up the sushumna from center to center, muhladhara to swadisthana to manipura to anahata to agna to sahasrara. As the energy moves from center to center reportedly greater powers of mind manifest and when this tremendous energy through the power of pranayama and

The Centers

meditation reaches the last center, the sahasrara chakra in the brain, the direct sensation of Self or Pure Consciousness is realized. It is called illumination or superconscious perception in which there is no limitation of self caused by mind or matter.

During some three years of meditation classes in which no effort whatever was made to move kundalini energy but only to lower energy to the naval center, we experienced tremors, vibrations, nervous twitches in the centers, as well as shaking, uncontrolled trembling with perspiration and internal body heat, manifesting primarily in the belly. A few people experienced rushes of energy up the spine but with no bad after affects. These phenomena have been occasional only and have felt rather pleasant after the initial shock wore off.

We have heard reports that Kundalini Yoga is dangerous and that practice without a teacher or without a perfect teacher can result in extreme mental disorder. The yogis can argue that there was something wrong with the student in the first place which caused the disorder such as incorrect diet, overemotional manifestations, excessive mental or physical tension, etc. We don't know of the dangers of yoga, if such exist. What is suggested here is that if Kundalini, Energy yoga, is your selected path, be careful indeed and proceed with caution. At least sit only before a Guru who has experienced what he teaches. Accept no substitutes.

Kundalini yoga thru Shakti Pat is a somewhat "cooler" path which may be of interest. It is based on the Pranic, psychic energy of the Guru. The Guru through initiation can start the arousal of the Kundalini energy in the disciple. Initiation can be accomplished as well thru an advanced disciple. Thereafter, the yogi practices love of Guru and relinquishment and the intelligent pranic energy of the Guru does the rest. The disciple will practice prayer, chanting, mudras, postures, bandhas, devotions and meditations automatically controlled by the Guru's Shakti energy. They are never injured in any way. The energy always seems to know precisely what is needed and when. In due time according to the nature of the individual, his spiritual evolution will be completed.

7

TIME AND PLACE

At this point we are undertaking to learn a formal practice of meditation. It is suggested that the practices of relaxation and inner awareness be exercised before proceeding. Experience is necessary so that the instructions that follow can be related to feeling-experience rather than as concepts to be recalled. Thus true learning proceeds faster. It is a fact indeed that like swimming one can learn more about meditation from an hour of practice than from reading a dozen books. Fear nothing, take courage and try.

A formal sitting period should be established for daily meditation. The period should start promptly each day at the same clock time. The main advantage is that it induces regularity in meditation and promotes the discipline necessary to continue. After practice has continued for some months one is called to meditation simply because when the time for sitting occurs one begins to relax, feels it and knows.

Regularity in meditation is vital for progress. Do not be deluded by moods prior to sitting. On days when one does not want to sit, the feeling may quickly pass, and the quality of meditation may be excellent. On the other hand when sitting is pleasantly anticipated, often a struggle ensues. In short when it is time to sit, sit. Sit methodically with regularity.

The time to sit depends on one's individual circumstances and when time is available. To sit in the morning has its advantages. For one thing, the world feels calm. It is generally quiet. Traffic noises are minimal. One feels refreshed from the nights sleep and the mind is generally quiet, not having recently been stimulated. On the other hand, waking may be difficult and drowsiness may plague one throughout. A definite advantage, quickly realized, is that the tone of the psyche is set for the day. One tends to be calm. It serves as a self-suggested reminder that one intends to be calmly aware regardless of what the day may bring.

To sit at night prior to retiring is a good time. The mind is quieter, sleep comes quickly and is restful. However it is noisier at night—traffic, dogs barking. The family is still awake—talk, radio and television are to be dealt with. The neighbors contribute their share of distractions. Additionally it takes longer to become established in meditation. Both mind and body have been stimulated by the days activities and it requires longer for the inner activity to subside. As always, final judgments rest with the meditator. One must try all periods and determine which is best for the individual.

Multiple sittings during the day are advantageous, one can sit both morning and night. Circumstances permitting,

Time and Place

short periods can be randomly practiced during the day. This works well for housewives, creative artists, and such.

A good rule is to sit as often as possible and stay as long as possible.

Sitting periods should never be less than twenty-minutes. When beginning, two twenty minute periods with a five minute break between seems to be adequate.

During the interval, stretch well. Sitting periods should be extended to forty minutes as soon as possible. Again, judge for yourself. Perhaps twenty minute sittings in the morning and thirty at night will be best for a while.

Any time is a good time. One can only meditate when one can.

Meditate with groups as often as possible but do your own thing. Practice your particular method. Be mindful in practice from moment to moment. Try to find a moment. What is the shortest instant you can find within you?

For the formal daily sitting try to sit in the same place. The surroundings themselves serve as suggestions to promote your meditation. Good meditators can practice anywhere but this is not so at first. Your bedroom or library will do. Your local church is an excellent place. It is often unused during the week and many rooms are usually available. The atmosphere helps. Find a place which is not too confining.

Natural surroundings are helpful because natural sounds do not tend to disturb, but bugs and weather can cause problems.

Do not locate specifically to avoid noise. Do not sit in noise proof rooms. Noise is more an advantage than otherwise. Once one learns to deal with noise it serves to rouse one from reverie and the exercise of imagination. Noise recalls the wandering mind.

The noise one can tolerate in meditation depends on the meditation. One can count breaths beside an active TV, meditate on the rise and fall of the abdomen beside the air conditioner but cannot meditate on subtle thoughts in the whisper of air-circulating fans. You will see for yourself and learn to adjust the practice. But generally speaking any place is a good place. The best time and place can only be determined by the meditator.

8

THE SEAT

All books on meditation place great emphasis on the meditation position, the seat. They go to great lengths to specify the details of the position. The seat is important and the reasons for a good seat should be made clear.

To begin with, the seat is a three pointed stable position of the human body centered on knees and rump with trunk erect. Deviations from an erect posture is discernable by virture of protesting muscles. A good seat is valuable for the neophyte meditator because it helps get something under control. A motionless body tends to quiet itself, and a quiet body promotes a quiet mind.

When the same position is assumed day after day it serves as a powerful suggestion to the mind that meditation practice is underway and the entire system tends to relax and prepare for the effort.

But most important of all is the fact that body and mind are not separate and during meditation mind and body interact. The condition of the mind is reflected in the position of the body. When mind is slack or wandering in imagination, body slumps, hands collapse, chin raises and body bends.

Understand—the body is used continually to alert the mind. Changes in body position recall the mind to awareness and reorient the mind to the awareness of the witness. As experience grows, body position is maintained by small unconscious corrections issued by a more continually alert mind. Ultimately the meditation seat becomes a position of comfort.

Place a folded blanket or pad about three feet square on the floor with a pillow about twelve inches in diameter and six inches high on the center of one edge. Place the buttocks on the edge of the pillow. Assume, say, the Half Lotus. Fold the right heel into the crotch and fold the left leg up onto the right thigh with the sole of the left foot up. Lean forward raising the buttocks. Reach behind with both hands and pull the pillow in tight under the buttocks. Raise the trunk erect with a slight arch to the back. Place the right hand palm up along the groin. Place the left hand palm up in the right, thumbs touching. From the front the fingers and thumb form an oval shape. This positions the arms outward from the sides. The arms do not touch the sides. Stretch the spine toward the ceiling, then settle the spine maintaining it erect. Let the shoulders fall naturally. Rock several times from side to side and backward and forward to feel for a vertical centerline. Look straight ahead, then bend the head forward to position the eyes on the floor some five feet in front of the seated position. Pull the chin in until the muscles on the side of the neck are stretched. The nose should be roughly positioned above the navel. Lower the eyelids to shade the eyes. Do not close the eyes.

The Seat

Close the mouth. Breathe through the nose. The tongue will rest quite naturally behind the upper teeth.

Now understand this: The meditation position is maintained by the *position of the chin*. When the balance point is correct a slight forward movement of the chin will cause the body to slump forward, a slight backward movement will cause the body to fall backward. The rule to a good seat is as follows: body erect, head erect, buttocks back, pelvis forward and chin in.

When terminating a period of sitting stop meditating, open the eyes fully and just sit for a few minutes looking around and reorienting. Rock forward head to the floor stretching the legs. Unfold, massage the legs and stand erect for a few moments. Sudden terminations are not recommended.

The pad need only be thick enough to cushion the knees and depending on the seat may not be needed at all. In the Easy Position the knees hardly touch the floor. Rather, one is supported by the flats of the legs.

Use a well padded pillow; as pillows compact during sitting the body lowers, stressing the folded leg. To compensate for the pain, the lower spine tilts backward, the body slumps, the back muscles take up the strain and discomfort ensues. Rather than a pillow one can fold up a rug to about six inches in height, placing a thin pillow on top. This arrangment will not compress and in fact may be an improvement over a standard meditation pillow.

It is not better to sit lower than higher. Experiment with pillows and establish what arrangement is best for yourself.

The position of the head is important. When lowering

the eyes do not bow the head. First bow the head then withdraw it to tuck in the chin. Experiment a bit, chin position is the key to a good seat.

Keep the mouth closed and breathe thru the nose. If you don't the mouth will become dry. Then it will be necessary to generate spittle by circulating the tongue between the lips and the front of the teeth and swallowing. It is said that if the tongue is placed behind the upper teeth it will act as a wick and conduct the saliva down the throat. This is not so. It is occasionally necessary to simply swallow. Do so mindfully and don't worry about disturbing your neighbor. It may be a help to him.

The eyes are not closed for several reasons. One squints to adjust the light entering to a comfortable level. When meditating outdoors in sunlight they may hardly be cracked or fully opened in a dark room. The eyes should be open so one knows how one is sitting. It is far easier to correct the seat if its orientation is known. Additionally, it prevents falling asleep and thwarts drowsiness in early morning and late evening sittings.

Finally, one's video imagery is not as intense and consequently not as difficult to deal with. Eyes closed, one tends to shift quickly in and out of the dream state. No one ever falls over backwards when meditating. The problem is forever slumping. The mind wanders, the chin lifts the body follows, slumping forward. The mind compensates by leaning further backward. The body curves, the muscles tire, etc.

As meditation progresses very often the crossed legs begin to ache. It is advisable to endure this for a substantial period by passively, intently "watching" the pain in all its variations. Generally the pain is relieved by unfold-

The Seat

ing the legs, conducting massage and resuming position. However, it is sometimes better to extend the protesting muscles even further simply by leaning forward for a short period, then returning upright.

The position of the hands is important and reveals to the meditator his present state of mind. When one becomes sleepy the thumbs (with hands held in Zen posture, hands palm up left hand in right and thumbs touching) pull apart. If one falls into dreaming the hands crumple inward. These are signals the teacher or monitor looks for during his rounds of posture inspection.

Five positions are suggested which will cover any physical limitations of the meditator.* They are presented below: the Full Lotus, the Half Lotus, the Perfect Position, the Straddle Position and the Seated Position.

The positions are shown in the order of decreasing dificulty. One should start with the most difficult position one can assume. An effort should be made to gradually work up at least to the position of Half Lotus. The reason is that the folded leg sets the back in a forward slant maintaining a slight arch which erects the back, tending to eliminate slumping. Nine times out of ten, the admonition "buttocks back, pelvis forward" will correct poor position.

* Photographs courtesy of Wellington Way.

The Full Lotus

To attain the Full Lotus position sit with legs outstretched before you. Take the right foot and carefully place in on the left thigh as close as possible to the abdomen. Take the left foot and place it on the right thigh as close as possible to the abdomen. Sit erect, head erect with chin in. Place hands as shown.

The Half Lotus

To attain the half Lotus sit with legs stretched before you. Take one foot and place the heel in the crotch. Take the other foot and carefully place it on the thigh as close to the abdomen as possible. Sit with back erect, head erect, chin in and hands as shown.

The Perfect Position

Sit with legs outstretched. Draw the left foot toward you and place the heel in the crotch, the sole resting against the right thigh. Insert the outer edge of the right foot between the left calf and thigh.

The Seat

Straddle Position

Place firm pillows in the center of a mat about three feet square. Pile the pillows up to about twelve inches. Straddle the pillows resting on the knees. Point the toes and extend the feet bottoms up and simply sit down. Keep the back and head erect with the right hand palm up, left hand palm up in right, thumbs touching.

Seated Position

If the foregoing positions are impossible, a stool can be used. Be sure to place a soft pad on the seat. The position is straightforward as shown. Do not use a chair. The back support to too tempting.

9

THE ATTITUDE

Attitude in meditation is very important. It can have considerable influence on one's progress or lack of it. At first, one is so busy simply getting the mechanics of meditation assimilated that it matters little, but later on looking for results can be truly inhibiting.

One has no purpose in sitting, one sits because one must. One sits for the sake of sitting alone and for no other reason. One does not sit to see reality as it presents itself. One does not sit to enhance extra sensory perception, nor to enhance awareness, nor to manifest phenomena, nor to induce trance, nor to have experiences, nor to condition, nor to decondition, nor to relax, nor to develop mediumship, nor to induce calm nor to attain enlightenment, nor to develop high energy, nor to obtain self-discipline, nor to stabilize one's emotions, nor to attain psychic powers, nor to etc. etc.

With few exceptions all meditations presented in what follows are passive in nature. Watch without opinion, without discrimination without conceptualization; thinking neither of good nor evil, accept whatever presents itself.

In meditation not only will you witness the object, you will hear sounds, see sights, feel emotions, and think thoughts. The technique consists in learning to back off and just look.

If, while watching the breath, a feeling interpreted as love presents itself back off and watch until it subsides. If the thought of a dear friend intrudes which caused the emotion, back off and watch it. If the mind begins presenting attributes of the loved one, back off and observe. When all subsides, return to the breath, refocus, and continue.

Encourage no thoughts support no thoughts, discourage no thoughts.

Sit in choiceless acceptance of the moment; nothing ahead, nothing behind, meditating for the sake of meditation alone.

10

DEALING WITH DISTRACTIONS

Do not be distracted by distractions in meditation and do not feel they are detrimental, for they are not—necessarily. They can be used to advantage. In a very real sense the whole art of meditation is the art of dealing with distractions.

How do distractions arise and what happens when one is distracted? Distraction is loss or displacement of attention, a sort of forgetting that one is concentrating on or focused on a particular object.

When one is centered on the breath then sounds, sights, feelings and thoughts are the primary sources of distraction. When centered on the breath both the witness and the breath are present in consciousness. When a motorcycle starts up outside, the mind hears, recognizes, and labels the sound, and in so doing forgets that it is watching the breath. By the time it remembers, it notices the lapse in attention and must be carefully returned to the object. The same lapse can be cited for sights since generally one meditates with the eyes open and the lights of a passing car shining through the window serves to distract. However, the real culprit is the conceptualizing mind. The mind continually presents random, tantalizing material for viewing which acts as a source for reviewing, problem solving, sensually fantasizing, recalling and planning and this must ultimately be confronted.

The mechanism by which the mind shifts from the object of meditation to the distraction is subtle indeed. More often one sees the return of the mind to the object rather than the shift to the distraction. Watch carefully.

There are three main ways of dealing with distractions, suppression, utilization and acceptance.

During the course of meditation, one can often anticipate the occurrence of a distraction, such as the sound of an approaching auto, or the refrigerator initiating its cooling cycle. One then clings to the object, say the breath, applying tension, bringing pressure to bear, deliberately forcing attention on the object and thus suppressing the distraction; that is, forcing it into the background. When the distraction subsides the tension, pressure, force is released and the mind gently held on the object.

The nature of some distractions make them more difficult to handle than others—familiar music, conversations, TV programs . . . When these occur, one may deliberately and mindfully direct one's attention to the distraction listening intently, continuously, without comment or concern. Again when the distraction subsides, patiently return to the original object of meditation.

Acceptance of distractions is a more difficult matter but ultimately is the best method and seems to be the natural result of experience in sitting. Regardless of the focus of the mind, data already interpreted is continually received and displayed. All sensory perceptions are simultaneously

Dealing With Distractions

occuring. The trick is to witness them all but to be simultaneously more aware of the object of meditation than the distractions. When sitting, watching the breath, you are in meditation so long as you are aware of the breath regardless of whatever other material is present. A sitter enters the meditation room late. Every sound is heard but the awareness of breath is continuous.

Treat distractions as a matter of fact. They are in fact—fact. They are phenomenal reality occuring from moment to moment and are, I'm told, noumenal reality as well—viewed aright.

How many times has a meditator been aroused from his daydreams and called to awareness by the growling stomach of the adjacent sitter? Never be afraid of disturbing your sitting friends by swallowing loudly. You may be waking them up.

How often has the sound of a pebble reflecting off a bamboo tree, the sound of a bird or the twinkle of the morning star led to Kensho or insight into Reality?

When distracted, patiently return to the work—without recrimination. The time may come when we learn that the only undistracted mind is an unthinking mind.

11

MEDITATION ON BREATH WITH COUNTING

Meditations on breath are the most common meditations found among the religions of man. They are found in Hatha Yoga, Mahayana and Theravadin Buddhism, as well as in Tibetan Buddhism and Taoist Yoga. They are both simple and complex, used for concentrating the mind energizing the chakras and moving energy internally. Breath meditations are generally used by beginners in meditation, and with good reason. The breath is ever present, readily found, linked to the autonomic nervous system, and presents an everpresent status of the emotional condition of the meditator. One is led to believe that breath meditations are easy since so often employed by neophytes. Don't believe it. There are no easy meditations, and in the end they are all alike—but different. In the end, the meditation you execute will be your own and no one else's. How could it be otherwise?

Much is heard of breath control and cyclic breathing. In these meditations, control is a dirty word. Nothing is controlled, simply monitored. Monitored is a good word. Such nonsense!

The breath is no simple thing. As a matter of fact it is no thing at all, to be found in no place. It is more a part of a process which we observe whose beginning and ending is not to be seen. Oxygen from sea algae is released to the atmosphere, carried by thermal imbalance on winds to one's vicinity, then inhaled. Carried by the blood to the cells of the body, consumed, rejected as carbon dioxide returned to the lungs and exhaled. It is inhaled by the nearest tree, mixed with sunlight, and exhaled as oxygen; then inhaled by a field mouse. Where is its beginning? Breathing makes strange bedfellows. Nevertheless we must begin.

The object is to concentrate the mind by hitching it to the breath, and as the breath quietens, the mind follows. Its value is that thoughts are stilled, the discriminating mind put to rest, and a gradual one-pointedness achieved.

To start, take an appropriate meditation position. Keep the spine erect, the head erect, the chin in, the mouth closed, the eyes open and breathe through the nose. Rotate the body around a bit to achieve a point of balance. Take several deep breaths and allow the breath to normalize, breathing through the nostrils.

- Do not attempt to stabilize the breath by deliberate shallow breathing. Simply watch and it will take care of itself.

- Focus the attention on the breath and let the witness arise in the mind. That is, be attentive to the breath while mindful of the fact that you are watching.

- Do not focus on any particular aspect of the breath but simply address the whole breath body. At this point it is enough to know that the witness is present, one is mindful of the breath, and that inhalations and exhalations are present.

Meditation on Breath With Counting

- Do not regulate the breath in any way and do not comment on it either. Simply note the inhalations following the exhalations.
- Maintain a passive observance and a non-critical awareness.
- On the next exhalation count one, witness the following inhalation and on the next exhalation count two and so forth to the count of ten. Then on the following exhalation count one, then successive exhalations to ten and repeat.
- Do not count aloud. Count with the mind. You will be distracted and forget the count. You will also overcount, eleven, twelve, thirteen. When you recover do not struggle to recall the count. Do not recriminate, simply return to number one on the next exhalation and begin again. Some professional basketball players practice dribbling eight hours per day so be patient and continue.
- As time passes, the breath will grow more shallow and subtle, and the mind will automatically add a number quietly and positively on each exhalation.

In the beginning, two twenty-minute periods of meditation with a five-minute break and stretch between is sufficient on a daily basis.

This meditation has the advantage that it gives a measure of concentration, since the number of lapses of attention are clearly discernable. When distractions occur, cling to the breath and to the count. Finally, skill will be achieved. It is important to recognize that you are in meditation when aware of the breath and mindful of the count.

12

MEDITATION ON BREATH

Meditation on breath without counting is generally more difficult because the mind is less occupied and more likely to become active seducing the meditator into the flow of mental activity. This, however, is not always so. For some, even in the beginning, the counting interferes with the meditator's concentration and makes the task more difficult.

To begin, the easiest way is to meditate on breath with counting and simply drop the count once established in meditation. As well, when meditation on breath is going "badly," it is useful to return to the count until the meditator feels he is "re-established."

Theravadin Buddhists speak of "investigative" meditation, a period of silent looking within to define the problem or to delimit or to surround. In short, to see what is really going on, rather than remembering what's supposed to be occuring according to some instructor's ideas.

A worthy meditation instructor will try to kick you out into the cold as soon as possible, to make you non-dependent and self-reliant. And if he really means it, you must trust yourself. No one really teaches meditation; the teacher suggests, the students learns.

Investigative looking should precede any effort in a new "technique," so look into meditation on breath.

Having established yourself in meditation with counting, drop the count when the breath grows subtle and without any effort whatsoever to control, successively focus the attention on the flow of breath in the nostrils, the throat, the lungs, in the rise and fall of the rib cage, in the rise and fall of the abdomen, and in the belly. Try then to see the total flow of breath, the whole "breath body."

When inwardly directing the attention, always refocus and move slowly and deliberately. Never jerk the attention around. Shift the attention from "point to point" in the breathing process until it can be done with ease and facility and a sense of awareness of the whole breath body is realized.

Another Buddhist idea with which it is advisable to become familiar is the concept of "attention." In this context attention means the simultaneous awareness of conditions "inside" and "outside," if there are such places.

Investigative meditation continuing then, sit in the woods where phenomenal activity is present and focus attention on the whole breath/body. Follow the inhalations and exhalations and while the awareness of the breath internally is continuing, be mindful or aware of the fact that you are seeing, i.e., the seeing process. Look without comment or opinion. Never lose sight of the breath or the seeing. Say that you are see-breathing. Similarly while mindful of the breath, close the eyes and listen intently. Do not objectify the sounds. Do not categorize, label or identify what is heard, simply hear-breathe. In the same way feel-breathe. While continuously aware of breath, feel the flow of air over the body, the pressure of the earth on the seat, the tickle of hair on the neck, the smell of mint, the

Meditation on Breath

taste of grass. In short, while aware of the breath, be mindful of sensory data.

It will not be long before a sense of integration manifests a sense of the truth, that we are not so separate from this universe after all. Another way of saying it—superimpose the breath on every aspect of life in the moment of meditation. Try to hold to the current breath exhalation after exhalation; none ahead and none behind.

Can you watch yourself breathe while you know you are thinking, reading or walking? Consider how you are really divided. Are the senses really separate from the breath or from each other?

Trust yourself. See for yourself. Trust no one else, It is better to disbelieve than to believe. It is better to look unjudgmentally than to disbelieve.

As for practice:
- Assume the meditation position.
- Take a few deep breaths and let the breathing stabilize.
- Meditate on breath with counting.
- Drop the count.
- Focus the attention on the whole breath body.
- Carefully follow the uncontrolled, unmodulated breath from inhalation to exhalation. Try to follow the subtle flow of breath.
- The body will grow calm.
- The mind will grow quiet.
- A tendency toward emptiness will manifest.
- Sense a continuous "thread of attention" between mind and breath.

- Where does the mind end and the breath begin?
- Wait quietly, expecting nothing, desiring nothing.
- Watch the breath in daily life particularly during periods of tension and emotional disturbances.

Meditation on breath can be utilized in most of the activities of daily life, promoting awareness and mindfulness of inner activity.

13

MEDITATION ON BREATH IN THE NOSTRILS

Meditation on breath in the nostrils is part of a system of mental training based on the Buddhas' "Way of Mindfulness." The method is used primarily in the Theravadin School largely in Burma and Ceylon.

This meditation is a good one for beginners and uses a specific object of meditation; breath in the nostrils rather than the whole breath body.

The practice begins by assuming a suitable meditation position with back erect, head erect, chin in, eyes open, mouth closed, breathing through the nose. The attention is directed to the flow of breath through the nostrils at the point where the breathing air strikes. The impact of the air in the nostrils is not continuous particularly at first when one is less sensitive to the flow. The impact of air is not felt momentarily at the point between the inhalation and exhalation nor for a rather lengthy period of time between the exhalation and the inhalation. That is to say, one pants when breathing, resting after exhalations. During the period when the impact is not present is the time when the attention is most likely to be seduced by the mind or other distractions. Things will go better if the attention is held firmly during that interval in the position in the nostrils where impact is anticipated on the following inhalation.

Try to tie a "thread of awareness," ever present, between the mind and the nose. Again the advice is emphatic. Do not interfere. Do not hold the breath nor slow the breath. Do not breathe deeply, shallowly nor rythymically. Simply, passively follow the natural flow of breath impacting the nostrils. Do not follow the breath into the body and out. That is not to say that you will not be aware of other aspects of the breathing process. Of course you will. Only be mindful of the fluctuations of the breath impacting the nostrils without concern with the total flow of breath.

Do not shift attention abruptly. Always move slowly and deliberately internally. The breath is not the enemy. Nothing to be overcome, nothing with which to compete. Remain calm and steady, no tenseness.

Regular, diligent practice, the key to success in all meditations, will lead to more sustained attention and greater detail in the architecture of the breathing process.

With experience, lapses of attention are fewer and more quickly noticed. As a matter of fact, when the meditator begins noticing breaks in attention, he is well on the way.

As awareness of the subtle aspects of breath manifests one will tend to divide breath up into a start, middle, and stop—ficticious of course but helpful in evaluating mindfulness. Subtly the mind can lead in anticipation, lag in delay or be synchronized with the flow of breath. One may thus evaluate the clarity of attention.

Watch without interruption the sequential flow of breath from inhalation to exhalation thru the impact in the nostrils. Set the attention in the nostrils and do not depart from that point of observation. Pay equal attention to all phases of the breath. Remain calm to the flow of the respiration and mental process. Float on the undulating flow without discriminating observations. Let the mind go silent, desire nothing. Simply observe.

14

MEDITATION ON RISE AND FALL

Meditation on the rise and fall of abdominal movement is the basic meditation of the Theravadin Buddhist Satipatthana or practice of Mindfulness. The practice itself is much like the meditation on breath in the nostrils and all those instructions apply here. Meditation on the rise and fall develops attention, concentration and eventually insight.

Rise and fall meditation is a good one for practice in daily life. It is a body centered meditation which places attention where the action is. The center of energy in the body resides in the lower tanjun, a couple of inches below the navel, the center of the emotions in the solar plexus just behind the movement. Energy in the body flows with the attention and in general the lower held the better.

When meditating on breath in the nostrils energy collects in the face and head giving a feeling of tension which leads to discomfort. Of course the occurence is occasional rather than continuous. Additionally the regular awareness of the rise and fall leads to a certain detachment from the body/mind and one is less likely to be overcome by, captured by, or lost in thought.

The object of meditation is the feeling of pressure resulting from the rising and falling movement of the abdomen. In order to locate the movement, lie on the back, breathe normally, place the fingers of one hand lightly on the abdomen just below the sternum, in front of solar plexus. Move the fingers around the area until the rise and fall of the abdomen is felt synchronously with the inhalation and exhalation of the breath. Feel the resulting pressure and remember its location.

Assume the regular meditation position with buttocks back and pelvis forward, spine erect, head erect and chin in until the muscles on the sides of the neck are in tension. Place the hand on the movement of the abdomen and lean backwards. Notice that the abdomen tenses and the motion ceases. Return to the upright position, locate the movement and lean forward. Notice that the rise and fall is emphasized. Clearly then an erect seat, continually held, is important in this meditation because the movement is affected by the body position.

Now direct the attention to the regular rising and falling movement of the abdomen. It is the object of meditation and is to be continuously observed. Take time to get familiar with the pressure movement before attempting the meditation proper.

Ignore what is said here. Assume you have been misled. Look for yourself. Follow the entire flow of movement. How does it go? Where is it located? What moves? What is felt? Where is the sensation? Investigate! Who is feeling?

Notice that the movement generally rises, falls and pauses, rises falls and pauses. See this. Verify it. Just as meditation on breath was initially supported by counting the rise and fall can be supported by labelling the flow initially. Thus one follows the natural flow of movement

Meditation on Rise and Fall

with the mental note rising, falling, sitting, rising, falling and sitting through the motionless interval. Try not to use the throat and subvocalize the labels. Simply put the tag on with the mind.

Similarly when one gets established in rise and fall simply drop the labels and follow the flow.

At first only the gross movements and pressure sensations are noticeable. As a result of persistent efforts in meditation refined features of the observed process become apparent.

Remember it is not the breath that is under observation, but the pressure sensation resulting from the movement.

Again, do not attempt to control the rise and fall in any way. Give bare notice to the physical process of movement without comment or special concern of any sort.

Again distractions will seduce the attention of the sitter. When this occurs, without recrimination return the attention to the rise and fall. When circumstances are not particularly conducive to meditation or concentration is poor, be flexible. Return to the labelling of the flow of movement, rising, falling, sitting, etc. until reestablished in meditation.

As meditation progresses awareness of the movement becomes unclear as the breath becomes shallow and the body quietens. At this time resort to a backup or secondary object. Simply know that you are sitting, i.e. as opposed to standing or lying down and correct the sitting position. Before long the movement will again become discernable and the sitter can return to his primary object of meditation.

Sit quietly for the sake of sitting. Insight manifests in its own time.

15

MEDITATION ON BREATH IN THE TANJUN

Sooner or later during the course of meditation practice one encounters the flow of energy. The energy, called that because it feels like energy, manifests not only internally but externally between people, plants and things. It is not necessary to meditate, either to manifest it or to be sensitive to it. Just what it is, its nature, is not clearly understood.

In the individual it feels as though one is filled with energy from the belly to top of the head. Heat may be present and the face flushed. Sometimes the face feels as though on *"pins and needles"* and seems to be *"radiating."* When the energy is "high" people and things, particularly plant life, seem to be "streaming" energy also. One then becomes very sensitive to energy in others. Often energy is exchanged between people by continuous eye contact and one can become so *"full"* it becomes difficult to breathe. Its' coming and going is often unpredictable, but manifestations of energy are often present when love is present, and the energy sensations are often interpreted as love.

How it is transmitted, if such is true at all, is equally mysterious. Certainly some people, more than others have the capacity to "turn on" others in their vicinity. Those *"turned on,"* sensitive to and later manifesting energy, come from all walks of life. They are no holier nor seemingly more *"ready"* than anyone else. It just happens, and once aware they tend to remain aware. It is not unusual to take up with trees or buildings or cars as a matter of fact. Some trees can really get one *"high."* For some it can easily turn into an *"ego trip"* and must consequently be dealt with.

The Indians speak of *"Prana,"* a universal energy or Life Force which is said to permeate *"phenomenal reality."* It is also called Shakti energy and is then said to consist of the intelligent psychic energy of a realized sage or guru which can be conferred on a chela and through a chela to others. The Prana has its counterpart in Chinese Taoism and is called *"Chi,"* the Life Elixir and in Japanese the well known *"Ki,"* utilized in the martial arts.

Korean Zen recognizes three main energy centers as significant, the upper, middle and lower tanjuns corresponding to the sahasrara, manipura and swadisthana chakras: that is the brain, the solar and the hypogastric plexuses respectively. In times of high energy, they do indeed seem to be interconnected and resonating or vibrating as a unit. Regardless of the concepts involved, the fact remains that ultimately energy will likely manifest within the meditator.

Yogic practitioners tend to carry the energy high in the body. That is in the solar and heart plexuses, the way of Zen, of Buddhism is essentially a *"cool"* path and the energy is carried low, in the lower tanjun. The lower tanjun is considered the main energy storage location or battery from which the energy is normally distributed to the rest of the body. Meditation on breath in the Tanjun or

Meditation on Breath in the Tanjun

belly concentrates the energy in that location. Hence the expression *"keep the belly hot and the eyes cool."*

Perhaps the concepts of acupuncture are good ones. They seem workable at any rate. Briefly, the acupuncture points, points of low skin resistance are apertures through which energy or life force flows into the body. Beneath the skin they are connected together by channels, called meridians, through which directed energy flows. The meridians terminate at one end in an internal organ such as heart, liver, lungs, or kidneys and at the other on the body surface such as the finger tips or the soles of the feet. The meridians are interconnected by other channels called sub-meridians and thus there is an internal body network for the flow of energy. The acupuncture points and meridians have been well known and charted for hundreds of years.

An examination of an acupuncture energy flow chart will show a complex of meridians, over the face and down the front of the body through chest, abdomen and belly. Perhaps with conscious effort energy can be made to flow along these from the top of the head to the belly. You can see for yourself whether or not this is so. Mediation on breath in the Tanjun involves the movement of energy along the flow lines from the top of the head to the lower tanjun, often referred to simply as *"the tanjun in the belly."* The tanjun is specified for location to be three inches or a finger's length below the navel. The specification of course is general. It is where it feels as if it is, at the point from which it responds to attention. Fundamentally, the fact is that energy in the body flows, and accumulates where, the attention is directed. Meditation on breath in the tanjun consists of lowering the energy to the tanjun, identifying the flow of energy in and out of the tanjun with the flow of breath while maintaining a passive observation of its occurence.

To begin with, assume the meditation position. Sit erect with the body pressure centered on the coccyx. Focus the attention on the tanjun in the belly. Feel in that place to the exclusion of the rest of the body. Pay no attention to noises. Keep the eyes closed and feel intently. Investigate a bit. Sharpen, narrow the focus of attention and explore the region of the belly. When any response such as an inner trembling or vibration or slight ache is experienced, maintain the focus at that point. If no response manifests, maintain the attention in the approximate position described. If one sits correctly the tanjun will be circumscribed by the oval described by the fingers and thumbs.

Now while the attention is held on the tanjun, the primary object of meditation, simultaneously be mindful of the breath. This will tend to center the breath in the tanjun, in the belly. Not only the abdomen rises and falls but the belly also though more slightly and this will help identify the breath there. Continue until the normal flow of breath seems to flow to and from the tanjun.

Again the imagination must be brought into play. While continuing to maintain the breath in the tanjun, extend the breath. Control the breath. Breathe rythmically. Use about one quarter of complete breaths. Continue to hold the attention in the tanjun with simultaneous awareness of breath and on the exhalation, note the **exhalation,** flow the breath **into** the tanjun. Always exhale **to** the tanjun. Only note the inhalation, giving it little importance and concentrate on the successive exhalations. Continue the practice until the tanjun is sensitive and the flow of breath into the tanjun on the exhalation and from the tanjun on the inhalation is clearly discernable, then slack off the extended breath and let it normalize. Remain in attendance to the tanjun and continue to sense the gentle flow of energy to and from the tanjun synchronous with the normal, unregulated flow of breath. Again the injunction, sit in passive awareness. Do not regulate the breath in any way. Merely sit. This constitutes the final *"condition"* for meditation on breath in the tanjun. All that remains is to first lower the energy.

To lower the energy, sit in the regular meditation position and focus the attention on the top of the head, on the scalp. Pay no attention to the breath. Breathe normally. Let the attention drift onto the forehead and slowly down to the eyebrows around the eyes and over the face to the upper lip, through the chin and down the front of the neck. Let the awareness spread out across the chest and about half way into the body, through the lungs and heart past the solar plexus and through the abdominals and into the waist. Continue the flow of awareness into the belly collecting it into a ball and placing it in the tanjun. Repeat this activity until the path of the energy becomes automatic. The path will define itself as it becomes sensitive.

The rate at which consciousness is lowered is slow, such as the rate at which molasses would flow down the body from the top of the head. In the beginning do not be too concerned with speed but try to feel the movement of energy and try to adjust to its motion. Visual imagery also can help as a temporary measure. For example, consider the body as filled with water and the plug pulled. Then the energy lowers with the water level. Any such device will serve.

Next enlist the breath to help. After some proficiency is established, inhale a complete breath and lower the energy in sync with the exhalation. Breathe the energy down. First from heaven, the top of the head, to the base of the throat. On the next exhalation from the top of the head to the solar plexus. Finally from the top of the head to the tanjun. In the beginning ten to fifteen minute sittings at this practice are sufficient then move on to the practice of breath in the tanjun. Ultimately the speed with which energy is lowered will depend on the long expulsion of a single breath.

Finally drop the use of imagination completely. Lower the energy by essentially pulling it out of the cells of the body along the sensible path of flow from head to tanjun in the course of the single, slow exhalation of a complete breath.

When proficiency is acquired, the lowering may be accomplished in a succession of three, six or nine breaths and one can meditate on the passive flow of energy to and from the tanjun in accordance with the normal breathing cycle.

This practice is different for different people. Some people have much energy, some little. In some it is difficult to move, in some, easy. Often the energy is easy to move in some places, hard to move in others. It tends to get hung up on the heart and solar plexus.

Do not be disturbed by vibrations or heat or slight nausea in the tanjun or solar plexus. If things get too intense, stop meditating or go to meditation on thoughts. When the energy is lowered and meditation is established just sit for the sake of sitting. All's well. Have you noticed how high energy in the solar plexus, heart and head is associated with fear, tension or emotional disturbance and the regular movement of the abdomen with serenity and calmness? The lower tanjun becomes a good place to be.

16

A BREATHING CYCLE

If we arbitrarily divide the human organism into breath, emotions, energy, body and mind and consider the breath centered in the whole breath body, the emotions centered in the solar plexus, the energy in the belly and the mind in the head, we can then cycle through the centers to monitor our general status and use the centers to modify or control our general condition.

Any position can be assumed at any time of convenience. Attention is focused on the breath is then controlled by extending the inhalations and exhalations. Use about quarter length breaths. Do not allow any discomfort in breathing to manifest. After about five minutes while maintaining attention on the breath, simultaneously become aware of activity in the solar plexus. Passively watch its condition which will yield a measure of the emotional excitation of the body. Do not attempt to control, simply watch.

After a few minutes, while maintaining breath awareness, shift the attention to the lower tanjun again passively observing the status of body energy. When established in the tanjun shift the attention to the entire body. Notice its position. Shift to one of comfort if necessary. Become aware of the entire body volume passing the attention throughout if necessary. Finally focus the attention on the volume of the head. Stand off from thoughts, simply noticing the activity, making no effort to control, while always being mindful of the breath. Return to breath-only awareness, and the cycle is complete.

If the personal condition is reviewed from day to day in this fashion, comparisons of status provide intelligence from which knowledge of the meditator can be deduced. As time goes on, more information of a subtler nature appears which becomes helpful.

One becomes aware of emotional upset, energy unbalance, tension in the body, and overactivity in the thought realm. One also becomes familiar with one's own patterns of inner activity which are then easier to deal with.

The patterns of inner activity, if undesirable, can be handled in the following fashion. Extend the breath and intently follow its flow. Focus attention on the solar plexus, or middle tanjun, and on the **exhalation** of the extended breath, flow the breath into the tanjun. Inhale naturally, and again, on the exhalation, flow the breath to the middle tanjun.

After three to five minutes or after the tanjun has "settled down" direct the attention to the lower tanjun. Here also flow the breath to the tanjun on the **exhalation** for a few minutes. This will have a calming, consolidating, lowering effect on the energy in the body.

Focus the attention on the entire body volume while being mindful of the extended breath. **Inhale** to the entire body, sensing the increasing body volume. Exhale naturally and repeatedly inhale to the body.

Focus the attention on the volume of the head and, as

A Breathing Cycle

with the body **inhale** to the head. Repeat for a few minutes and allow the "mind" to flow with the breath.

By cycling the breath in this fashion the organism is calmed and grows serene. The exercise can be performed following any trying circumstance and grows more effective with each repetition. Remember, after a short period of attention to the breath, flow the breath on **exhalations** to the middle and lower tanjuns and on **inhalations** to the body and head.

17

WALKING MEDITATION

A walking form of meditation was used in China during the Chan period and is currently used in Japanese and Korean Zen. It is used as well in Theravadin Buddhism. It is used for short periods, about fifteen minutes, between sitting meditation periods of about forty minutes in Zen meditation halls.

In a Zendo the altar is usually located at one end of a rectangular room and customarily the students sit on cushions or meditation pads facing the walls along the other three sides. At the sound of a bell meditation ends and the student bows while seated. A clapper sounds and the students rise, step toward the wall, turn left and so are in file. They assume a position in which the right thumb is grasped in the left fist and the right hand folded over it. The hands are placed on the sternum and arms extended laterally, parallel to the floor. The head monk then leads the procession around the Zendo. On occasion he will exit the building circling the Zendo to return later. He will circle the Zendo within and stop the file with the clapper and each student will be positioned before his meditation seat.

At the sound of the clapper each will resume his meditation position and at the bell resume Zazen.

The pace varies from running in China and some Japanese Rinzai temples to very slow half steps in Theravadin custom. In Korean Zen the pace is moderate and is very slow in the Soto sect. A few statements may help in regard to this practice. First, it is important to maintain the same meditation practice employed when sitting. This means you must let more in without being distracted from the object of meditation. The body will be protesting from a long period of motionless sitting and the student in front will be changing gait so it helps to walk duck footed with toes pointed outward at forty five degrees. When walking the weight comes forward to the front leg and the rear heel is raised with each step. The protesting stiff muscles and the slow pace tends to cause falling to the side. The walking period is refreshing but it must be a period in which the mood, sense, thread and continuity of the sitting period is not lost.

18

THE CONFRONTATION

Lord Buddha has said in the Dhammapada, *"You are what you are because of what you have thought in the past. It is founded on your thoughts. It is made up of your thoughts."* In so doing he pointed directly at the core of our predicament and placed the responsibility for our *"salvation"* directly on our own shoulders. By no stretch of the imagination can we believe that anyone but ourselves can deal with our own thoughts.

We spend the majority of our days vainly attempting to elude the pain and exploit the pleasures produced by them as a result of our interpretation of our perceptions. We all know of the courage we lack in *"swallowing the West River,"* in looking directly at ourselves *"accepting the good and the bad."* The fact is that when we face ourselves directly we face a mess indeed. We perpetually recall our past sins, failures, lacks, and short comings. And if that were not enough, we perpetually torture ourselves with conceptual failures and insecurities in a dreamed of future which will never exist. To add to all this we find that our thoughts are disorganized, unpredictable and random in occurrence. So what do we do? We run away. We avoid painful thoughts. We think not. No blame is intended here. We are so trained from birth; so conditioned. How often have we heard praise for the *"goal oriented"* achiever? Always the cries resound, consume, enjoy, participate, become involved, play the game, compete, win, achieve, drink, party and work. And let those who wish, so respond. But for some, the goal of life must be to find an answer to the enigma of man, the ultimate koan echoing in the silence: *"What is this?"* To answer this, one must deal with his own mental construction of himself; his thoughts, the symbols that stand in lieu of him.

The meditations that have been presented thus far are admittedly *"techniques"* in which an *"I"* attempts to achieve a condition. They are intensive, awareness contracting meditations which tend to make the mind silent by excluding reality in part and by ignoring thought. The meditations which follow, Hua Tou and Chigwan Taja, are extensive meditations which tend to expand awareness and let more in. They involve the direct confrontation with thought and consequently with what we are to date.

You do not think you are made up of thoughts? Then ask yourself the question, *"Who is my best friend"?* Write a statement of your understanding. Then ask, *"Who am I"?* Write that statement also. In both cases you will have listed the qualities of an object and your opinions concerning it. There will be few differences, merely a matter of detail. And are the statements not simply recorded thought sequences? If the exercise were repeated six months later would not the descriptions change? Can we not see here that our phenomenal nature is **symbolic** and that furthermore the symbols are transient and ever changing? Are we not indeed made up of our thoughts? If we can see this then we can at least take consolation in some progress. By recognizing the symbolic nature of thought,

The Confrontation

of our phenomenal selves as thoughts that *"stand in lieu of"* reality, a substitute for reality, perhaps we can begin to cope. Perhaps what we are is beyond thought and all the while we have been accepting a phantom for ourselves.

If we turn to science, to psychology for help in understanding what we are, we find just as much of a mess as when we look within. Instead of the study of the psyche, the determination of a working concept of mind verified in human experience, we find "schools of thought" or sects such as Freudian, Gestalt, Behavorial, Existential, Psychoanalytical or Reality psychologies which emphasize method since results are scanty. Our mental "problems" are here and now, so we must look for ourselves in the present.

Concepts of mind divide us up into conscious, superconscious, subconscious, and collective unconscious minds; into id, ego, superego; into thoughts, feelings and emotions.

Where are these entities when we look within? No such separate things even appear to exist, the relationships among them not apparent so that nothing practical or helpful can be derived. No place is there ego, no place emotion. There is no correspondence, so what recourse have we?

A practical approach seems to be one of self discovery by pattern recognition. Let us not divide ourselves into a piecemeal, fractional being, but wordlessly examine and become familiar with our patterns of function. Continuous self examination sooner or later leads us to the conclusion that ultimately we are all of a piece and that clearly no fractionalization exists.

The Buddhist fourfold concept of man, for purposes of convenience, divides man up into body, feelings, state of mind and contents of mind. For state of mind, read emotions; for contents of mind, read thoughts. The inference is that emotions are mind and not separate therefrom and such truly seems to be the case. Lets take a look at the pattern of extreme emotion within.

Let us say that the thought of a person arises who has done us a personal injury. This causes a corresponding feeling to arise in the belly and solar plexuses. The feeling is interpreted as dislike and causes the mind to dwell on the subject. Fantasy ensues in which the injury is recalled and dramatized causing energy to rise in the belly and feelings of greater intensity in the solar plexus. In turn the fantasy intensifies. Roles as designed and played by the mind are then revised, edited and replayed. This positive feedback drives emotion to the extreme and we are hating the enemy. The horror of it all is that it happens automatically and very rapidly and we are lost, and in fact we are **in** hatred and **out** of control.

The pattern is a very common occurrence and once pointed out is not too difficult to see. Love, works in much the same way. The thought of a loved one arises, recollections of pleasure and the loved one manifest. Feelings arise and are interpreted as loving; energy rises, fantasy intensifies and love obtains. Is it necessary to review the sequence of sexual excitation? It is important in observing the process to note that the patterns are repetitive and integral. In short it must be viewed as a pattern of experience recognized as such at a non-verbal level. One can observe that emotions are less determined by feelings than by the contents of mind. The feelings are pretty much the same but interpreted differently by thoughts as all paint is the same except for pigmentation.

The mechanism of worry and tension is the same. To

The Confrontation

discover the cause, it is necessary of course to watch the associated thoughts.

The mind is a sensual organ always desiring and seeking gratification, assurance and security. If we are unaware, the mind will have us off on some errand or another to satisfy its needs continually. We indeed rarely act on impulse. The thought almost always precedes the action.

So we've learned to observe the psychosomatic patterns within. What can be done to control the behavior which follows? It has been said that if we do not control the mind, it will surely control us. Without control we are automata and deliberate living is impossible. Is it not so? **To effect control, watch. Do not participate. Do nothing! The most important thing to note is that the process is transient. It has a beginning and an end. Eventually it is over. Just wait. Do not respond in any way!**

Somehow watching drives a wedge between the thought and feelings and the pattern subsides. One learns that one can always wait it out. Additionally, familiarity with the process leads to control without controlling. When we begin to see that hate and anger are patterns within ourselves and the hated object remains unaffected, as soon as we see the pattern arise, it begins to lose its force. After watching the patterns of emotional behavior day after day, the time comes when we've had enough. We become bored with it all.

Other patterns require examination such as fantasizing, mental activity in problem solving, the loss of awareness in daydreams and action. **Recognize** the patterns. Don't **analyze** them.

An important effect that this practice produces is to smooth out our emotional lives. There are fewer high and lows and the middle path is nearer. In any case we can choose our emotions.

We must see that some patterns are painful and others are pleasant. Regardless of our opinions we must not run neither toward pleasure nor from pain. We must look all the action in the face, see it directly and accept the bad with the good. After a while we begin to wonder what on earth we have been running from. The pain was never that intense from the very beginning.

Watch in silence, know that it will surely pass. Don't participate. Take courage. Now we know how to look!

19

MEDITATION ON THOUGHTS

If the struggle for Realization, the Enlightenment of a Christ or a Buddha can be considered a game, albeit the Mastergame, then the arena in which the contest is held is in the mind in direct confrontation with our predicament. If we are what we are because of what we have thought in the past then our future depends directly upon what we are thinking in the present and from that we can take heart. To see Reality clearly we must *"drop the baggage,"* void all concepts and somehow transcend or go beyond thought. Hua Tou, thought head or ante-thought meditation is a direct attack on the problem. *"Be Still and Know"* does not mean to remain motionless—but to think not and know. Only in silence can Reality appear.

Meditation on thoughts in no way implies the suppression of thought. For us, the unrealized, it is simply a way of letting the mind go silent and waiting to see what happens next. One observes the mind in tranquility never supporting, participating or opinionating and letting it run down out of a lack of fuel rather than through the application of effort.

The transition from breath meditations to meditation on thoughts is always difficult unless the student has been meditating for a long time and has dealt with the problem of thought disturbances. In thought meditation the object of meditation is in no way as obvious as breath nor as regularly occurring. Thoughts vary in kind and are randomly occurring, far more subtle and difficult to follow. Consequently it is easier for the mind to become distracted.

If we are to meditate on thoughts, it is certainly necessary to know the kinds of thoughts we have and where to look for them. All that can be done here is to attempt to relate experience resulting from meditation and hope that it can be of use.

For convenience, thoughts are divided into audio, directly perceived, video and intuitive categories.

Audio thinking occurs in the throat and in the head. When we say that we are thinking very often we mean to say that we are talking to ourselves. We spend much of our time doing this. It is easy to see this occur and it is only necessary to look in the throat. With just a little practice one can shut off the talk. Do not do so in meditation. Let it all hang out. Do not interfere.

One hears sounds in the head in just about the middle of the head. When one is not talking to oneself in the throat one is often doing so in the head. To know that words are presenting themselves in the head, it is not so much a talking as in the throat as a hearing.

Directly perceived thinking, consists of directly sensing thought prior to interpretation by the mind. In the back of the head a sensation occurs, an impulse as though a data package has arrived. This is often followed by an exclamation such as "I understand" or *"I get it"* or *"I have an idea."* So lets call it an idea. The significance is that considerable information is contained in that impulse or idea

Meditation on Thoughts 107

which has not yet been translated into words or pictures or combinations thereof. But then the mind begins delineating sentence after sentence until the translation is complete. This is not uncommon. You can see for yourself. It is like thinking in paragraphs. The point is that the arrival of information can be sensed in the head with a rather unique feeling before it is translated into words of information.

When all is silent the reception of words, data in the head, can be clearly perceived. The sensations are felt in the back of the head and presage the coming of words. Repetitively words are received, translated and announced. With careful observation you can experience this. One can even play games here. As the sensations of the reception of words occur one can cut off the translation, suppressing thought or sit in the interval of translation watching for the results or even cut short the translation trying to understand the information's content without allowing the translation to occur. However, in meditation do not interfere in any way. Thoughts don't really amount to much do they? One can hardly say that these transient, biological impulses are either good or bad. Nevertheless it is on the basis of these impulses that we make all judgements.

Video information or pictorial data or visual imagery tends to manifest in the front of the head behind the forehead as though looking at a movie through frosted glass. Sometimes it seems as though the image is outside the body. You will not have much difficulty discovering where to look within yourself to see this.

Intuitive thinking is difficult to describe. First it is spontaneous. It is sensed by the entire body. It is not expressed in audio or video. It constitutes an intense sensation of knowing. As well, one perceives considerable information in the process, seeming to become the information oneself. Sometimes it seems as though one is sensing outside the skin. This is not often encountered in meditation but is included here in the hope that it may be of some help.

See for yourself! Do so now. Focus the attention on the breath and watch carefully until the breath becomes finer and the mind quietens. Look in the throat and wait until you begin talking or singing to yourself. If you grow impatient, recite a poem without moving your lips. Mary had a little lamb. Then stop. When you begin to subvocalize, note the sensation and the place of occurence.

Transfer the attention to the middle of the head where you hear words. Very often these are the very words that are subvocalized and are often simply repeated when you speak. Watch carefully, try to see words come and go. When one is seen, watch it end and look for the next. Be patient. Sometimes the very looking tends to inhibit the flow of words but never fear we can't be silent for long. Think, not speak, your name to yourself repetitively. Watch the words appear in the head. Mark carefully the sensation and the location of the occurence of the word thoughts.

Look further back in the head. Be very still and quiet. Try to feel an impulse or thought sensation and the word following it. Feel intensely for the sensation. Again, repeat— think your name. Try to follow the word back into the mind to see where it comes from. Do so for a few minutes then stop thinking your name but keep looking. Usually the mind continues to run on like a broken record for a while and sometimes then you can see the process; sensation, word, sensation, word, etc. Do not be dismayed if you find this difficult. If you practice thought meditation you will experience this sooner or later. It is an advantage in meditation to know in advance that words are arriving.

Meditation on Thoughts

If you can look back this far then meditation automatically deepens.

The only difference between words and ideas are the data content. The sensation is the same. With practice, you will see.

Look in the front of the head and watch for imagery, visual thought. Visualize an apple or a loved one or a telephone. Mark the sensation and location of the imagery. Is it in technicolor or black and white? Visualize the scenery along the drive from work to home. Watch carefully.

Circulate through the locations from time to time; vocalizations in the throat, words in the head, the sensation of the arrival of data and on to visual imagery. Look into the mind during daily activity and grow familiar with the kinds of thoughts occurring and the circumstances in which they occur. All that is asked here is that one observe the thought process. Why is it that words in the head are called thoughts but hunger pangs in the belly are not?

Intuitive thinking is found by accident. If one can wander through a crowd or a forest observing silently with a quiet mind, knowledge comes sometimes. Buildings, trees and fields sometimes have things to say. Often we know what a person intends to say before he speaks. Be ready, be silent and watch. Sit in a place of beauty, in natural surroundings. Look at a tree. At the first comment or observation, at the first labelling, move on to another object, say moss on a rock. Again at the first expression of opinion move on. Continue until the mind tires of the game and refuses to comment. Then dwell on the object and wait for knowledge.

Up until now in meditation we have been following manifestations of breath with the mind's eye. Now we must follow the mind with the mind's eye. To do so is quite difficult so the correct temper of mind is important. We must be supremely patient, unhurried, firmly planted, massively composed and perservering. We must be continually aware and never relax vigilance.

As for practice:
- Assume the meditation seat.
- Let the witness arise in the mind.
- Know you are observing.
- Lower the energy to the tanjun.
- Meditate on the lower tanjun until established in meditation until the mind quiets down.
- Look into the body until it becomes silent.
- Shift the attention to the head and circulate through the locations where thoughts normally occur.
- Focus on word thoughts. The throat talk will stop. Visual imagery will occur occasionally. If thoughts are streaming, let them go by, simplying observing as of a train at a crossroad. Try to see the arrival, stay and departure of thoughts.
- When you have isolated a thought apply pressure and watch for the ending. Hold the attention through the silent interval watching for the start of the next word. Watch its arrival, stay, and departure. Again dwell in the interval and so continue from thought to thought.
- Pay no attention to the *content* of the words.
- Do not support the thoughts in any way.
- Do not have thoughts about thoughts.
- Let them occur naturally, flow as they will.
- Again, see them word by word and never, never respond in any way.

Meditation on Thoughts

- Make no attempt to control thoughts.
- When the attention is lost or shifts to another object such as outside sounds, as soon as awareness returns, redirect attention to the next thought occuring and begin again.
- Never recriminate for loss of attention. As meditation progresses, thoughts become fewer and the silent interval grows longer, look back further into the mind and try to sense the arrival of the words.
- Watch the sequence of arrival sensations and the words which follow, always returning to the sensations and the words which follow, always returning to the sensations when attention is lost.
- Finally merge with the background from which thoughts emerge holding attention primarily on the *silent interval between thoughts.*
- Sit patiently in the field of consciousness permitting the flow of thought to emerge from you, to occur within your being. As the silence becomes more prolonged, sit in the silence wanting nothing, desiring nothing.

During the course of thought meditation tension may build up and energy may accumulate in the head. Headaches may occur. If so return to meditation on the lower tanjun until the condition is alleviated. Do not feel that your meditation must strictly follow what is presented here. You will naturally develop your own methods.

This meditation requires months to acquire proficiency but it is a very powerful one indeed. It is very satisfying in the sense that one truly begins to know oneself. With familiarity one becomes predictable.

Sooner or later the problem of loss of attention must be faced. Meditation manuals say "the mind runs away" or "awareness is lost" which says nothing. The occurence is a subtle thing indeed and must be looked for incessantly. It is in thought meditation that we view the problem directly.

In meditation mindfulness must always be present, that implies the witness or watcher and the object, the thing watched. Both the witness and the object are directly sensed. One can observe either. Both must be present for awareness to be present. The witness directs attention to the object. Awareness is lost when either the witness or the object is lost. It is as though both are only thoughts, the witness coming and going just as any other thought. In meditation, loss of attention occurs in at least the following ways:

- The witness is lost. One simply forgets that he is meditating. The witness thought stops.
- The object is lost. The mind simply, automatically switches to another object. When watching the tanjun one suddenly observes that one is instead listening to an outside sound.
- Supportive thinking occurs; an automatic process. The witness thought vanishes. One has thought of a heat transfer problem. The mind then sorts out all the functional relationships necessary to solve it—a result of training. One "awakes" in the middle. This is the kind of thing referred to as "asleep though awake."
- Fantasizing occurs. The witness thought departs. The mind writes a play, creates the actors, their roles, and executes, taking all the parts itself, supplying the settings and speaking the lines. Emotions are also injected as needed. Again, a habitual thought pattern manifests. When the witness thought arises, again we awaken.

Meditation on Thoughts

- Sometimes the witness thought seems to be attenuated, intensity diminished, by a heavy stream of words or intense imagery after which we recover, but the witness was not quite gone. We can still vaguely remember we were watching and can still remember the thought sequences.
- Finally, we go to sleep. In meditation as all quietens it seems as though we are getting ready for sleep and so sometimes we shift in and out of dream. It is strange indeed if one dreams in technicolor. One always "knows" one is dreaming when color is present.

Perhaps too much has been said here concerning meditation on thoughts, and all can be summed up in the clear, simple directions of Zen Master Song Ryong Hearn: "The illusory *"I—self"* dies when *"the mind is caught,"* so we say. Watch patiently, steadily, the point where thoughts emerge. Watch carefully and go to the very bottom. When there is only stillness, watch that which watches *"outer"* sounds. Then the real *"Mind-flower"* bursts into bloom and the years of slavery to an illusion are finished. You will be free."

20

A MEDITATION

One sits.
The witness arises.
One surveys the body, feelings, emotions and thoughts.
One fixates on the whole breath body.
The body relaxes.
The seat is adjusted.
Feelings diminish in intensity, become fewer.
The light softens.
The energy lowers.
The breath settles, becomes finer, more regular.
Concentration improves. Attention is held to the natural flow of breath continuously.
Time passes.
Distractions fade into the background of the mind.
Body noises grow louder; the digestive process, the heartbeat.
The breath grows very subtle.
One is established in meditation.
Attention is transferred to thoughts.
All thoughts are seen at once.
A thought as a word is perceived.

It is watched carefully, clung to, followed back to its origin as it decays.
The silent interval is seized and that voidness held in awareness.
One watches alertly for the next thought. It starts, sustains, decays. Again the interval is grasped.
The experience; thought, interval thought, interval etc. continues.
Occasionally sounds are heard, one yawns, the legs protest, but always in the background.
Meditation is continuous.
Time passes.
The body stiffens.
The breath becomes shallower.
Thoughts reduce, the silent interval increases.
Thoughts become subtler, softer, more difficult to perceive.
One works harder and tries to feel behind the thoughts to sense their arrival.
Sensations of the arrival of thoughts are perceived. The thought is felt before it forms a word in the mind.
The word follows; the sensation, the interval, the word, the sensation, the interval, the word, etc.
One relaxes and watches the process, distractions coming and going.
Repetitiously one returns to the work; the sensation, the interval of interpretation, the word.
Time passes—
Thoughts become even fewer and the thought of the witness becomes more insistent, clamoring for attention. The witness drifts and sits like a mask behind the face and attention must be forcibly returned to the place where thoughts emerge.
Now thoughts and the witness are well contained.
Mindfulness is continuous, awareness uninterrupted.

A Meditation

Distractions are remote and ineffectual.
One borders on sleep.
Suddenly fixation shifts just slightly behind the thoughts.
   Instead of watching the thought process, one seems to focus on the background of consciousness, as a screen or voidness from which thoughts emerge as though from oneself.
The mind becomes like a mirror reflecting all phenomena; thoughts, sounds, breath, heartbeat and discomforts with equal weight. All phenomena have the same value.
A further shift occurs and it seems as though one is the consciousness in which all phenomena manifests, transiently coming and going. One speaks here, sounds there, feels elsewhere; but all of a piece—warp and woof of the same fabric. Momentarily body and mind, inside and outside fall away.
One just sits:
   Without motive.
   Without desire.
   Without thought of gain.
   For the sake of the sitting.
"Does this help?"

21

CHIGWAN TAJA MEDITATION

Descarte had a profound effect upon the Western philosophers of his day when he declared, *"I think; therefore I am."* It was as though he had somehow logically verified the existence of man's individual identity. The truth of the statement, even on a logical basis is questionable. Logic is a system of thought which defines a relationship among variables. If A then B, where A is thoughts and B is *"I."* A and B are just containers for objects. One could say, if heat then sweat. The point is, that such premises must be tested. A equal to thoughts exists alright but where is B, an *"I"* to be found?

Oriental philosophers would have been much more impressed with his insight into Truth had he said, "I do not think; therefore I am not." Or even, *"I do not think; therefore 'I' am."*

Chigwan Taja of Korean Zen or the Japanese 'Shikan' is a total awareness meditation which implies the absence of ego in the very practice. In the beginning the meditator feels separate from the object of meditation. The "witness" is developed which serves as a point of awareness from which the flow of circumstances, thoughts, sensations and feelings are viewed. Later total unity must be reached in which the observer and thing observed are united in pure motiveless, mindful sitting. Sitting is present but the sitter has vanished. Being becomes unified and split-mind has become whole-mind.

Buddha, it is said, studied with teachers throughout India in an effort to solve the problem of life but without success. Finally he simply let go of thought and the intellect, and Reality just naturally appeared in glowing, timeless silence. He saw that Reality was a whole piece of cloth without a single seam, and that people and things exist in an inevitable relationship of undivided oneness. It was clear that Enlightenment was no "special" state but was the natural condition of man.

Chigwan Taja is no beginner's meditation. Both extensive practice of meditation and real understanding are necessary. One is instructed to sit and simply dwell in the relationship with surrounding circumstances without thought of good or evil until the observer disappears. But that is no easy thing to do.

If we have not practiced extensively, we will neither be able to concentrate properly nor to look aright. In Chigwan there is no thing which is not the object of meditation. As a result one is bombarded with impulses and sensations from all directions and is soon overcome. One must be able to "take in" a flux of conditions at a glance without loss of awareness. Chigwan is a total awareness meditation.

Some real understanding is also necessary. Words divide reality into pieces which do not separately exist. Yet because we think it so, we behave as though it were so. We are a total, undifferentiated organism in which everything "thinks." Because "thoughts" occur in the head we say the

Chigwan Taja Meditation

mind is located there and give special value to those thoughts rather than say, hunger in the gut.

Recent evidence indicates the entire organism is thinking. For example, Russian experiments recently have shown that poisoned human tissue cells, when dying, communicate with other unpoisoned cells of the same variety which die sympathetically. The means of communication is probably through modulated ultra violet light. The decision to die was made at the cell level. The problem was not submitted to some "mind" which then directed the cell behavior. Again, one hears the sound of a ticking clock, the sound disappears. We no longer hear. It is just because we are not concentrating on it, right? Not so! The sensor, the ear, does not transmit the vibrations resulting from the ticking clock to the brain. The ear, the sensor "decides" at the sensor level that the information is not important and filters it. But if the intensity or rate of the clock changes the ear will again transmit. Aren't ears smart? The body/mind schism just isn't so.

The universe consists of electromagnetic radiation of various phases, intensities and wavelengths; flowing, vibrating, air molecules; varieties of gasses; accumulations of atoms of various configurations and densities; and in direct participation, perfectly executing, the organism constructs a symbolic universe consisting of light, color, form, sound, taste, feel, heat, breath, etc. No thing exists which is not our own integral mental construction. Physically and "mentally" we are one with the universe—until we begin to think. Thought separates. The inside/outside schism just isn't so. The view of reality as a totality is most obvious in the practice of Chigwan in which one views without opinion, the Tao, the flow of circumstance.

One can work one's way into Chigwan. To begin look

into the lower tanjun. In so doing look "through the body," be aware of the body and the contained feelings and emotions. Set the awareness to be ever mindful of the status of feelings. Simultaneously attain awareness of "outer" sounds neither pursuing or evaluating but observing both inner and outer. While observing feelings and sounds be mindful of sights. Try to see them as a continuity of perception. Conduct this practice outside in the quiet of dusk and let inside and outside merge. One readily learns that external circumstances and their effect on the organism merge into a total experience and the assumption of separation diminishes in intensity. This tends to heal the inside/outside split.

Similarly sit quietly and again look through the body to the tanjun and set the awareness to experience feelings. While mindful of feelings, pay attention to the contents of mind. In short watch the feelings while you think. A continuation of this practice tends to develop a thinking body. This tends to heal the body/mind split.

To sit in Chigwan Taja, then, focus attention in the lower tanjun and attend the feelings. Subsequently add sounds, then sights then thoughts. Work hard. Sit passively but let nothing escape notice and make no attempt to attain any special state. Let things happening around and within, happen freely.

It has been said that ego exists only as an image of thought. Perhaps we can see this fact in the practice of Chigwan and save ourselves by letting go of the thought of ourselves.

Perhaps the spirit and practice of Chigwan can be summarized in the aphorisms of Wei Wu Wei:

"All I am is seeing when I see—no seer, nothing seen.

All I am is hearing when I hear—no hearer, nothing heard.
All I am is sentience when I feel—no feeler, nothing felt.
All I am is understanding when I know—no knower, nothing known."

22

MEDITATION IN DAILY LIFE

Meditation, at first a trial, becomes a joy and then a vital necessity. Many anticipated as well as unexpected benefits appear. For some this is not enough and the need for Realization grows more insistent. If we look at the regimen of a Zen Temple we find that students meditate formally from six to ten hours daily depending on the season. We ask ourselves, "How can we do less?"

The problem presented is difficult indeed. First we haven't the time. Secondly the stress of the wordly life seems to quickly undo the progress we make in our meditations. Somehow or other we must remain in meditation such that there is no difference between a formal sitting on a pillow or driving the car to work or buying a newspaper. In short we must extend our meditation into more and more of our daily activities.

One way is to make a list of rules and discipline oneself to abide by them. For many this is very difficult to do and tends to intensify ego—I am this way—I must become that. The effort is to polish a ghost, to bring "oneself" into conformance with a mental model. No doubt about it, though, some rules must be followed.

To find a way to do this one can experiment with each daily acitvity and apply some meditation to it, such as watching the rise and fall while brushing the teeth or lowering the tanjun when getting angry. This is like meditation by various devices.

What we are trying to work out now is a system of internal management plus adherence to some rules which naturally follow. The method implies that one permits oneself to exist in only one of four internal conditions: breath in the belly, inside/outside, body/mind and total awareness. This is essentially Chigwan Taja in daily life.

Breath in the belly is meditation on breath in the lower tanjun. The energy is lowered to the tanjun and the breath allowed to normalize. Attention is held in the tanjun and breath, "prana" flowed to the tanjun on the exhalation. One body breathes.

Inside/outside is meditation which first centers or references breath in the belly, and once established, one simultaneously hears all sounds and sees all sights. One registers thoughts but does not respond. **One body looks.**

Body/mind meditation also references breath in the belly and takes in all the feelings in the body as one looks through to the tanjun. Simultaneously, one watches all thoughts. **One body thinks.**

Total awareness meditation references the tanjun and simultaneously looks and thinks. The entire organism centered in the tanjun is aware of all incident stimuli and inner phenomena.

Thereafter one relates one of the conditions to some daily activity for example: one rests or idles in the breath in belly mode, one drives in total awareness mode, one listens in inside/outside mode one studies in body/mind mode.

No matter what the "mode," one is conscious at all times of the condition of the tanjun.

- One acts from the tanjun.
- One breathes in tanjun.
- One moves in tanjun.
- One sits in tanjun.
- One angers in tanjun.
- One speaks in tanjun.
- One listens in tanjun.
- One energizes in tanjun.
- When breathing, know it.
- When standing, sitting, lying down, know it.
- When walking, know it.
- When emotional, angry, sad, loving, worried, know it.
- When speaking, know it.
- When looking, know it.
- When feeling, know it.
- Awareness, mindfulness is the key.
- Maintain a thread of awareness or continuity of attention through everything you do.
- Remain attentive to the method employed.
- Keep the goal in view.
- Execute all duties with detachment.
- Don't be too elated with success or dejected with failure.

- In times of stress learn to interrupt, pause, clearly comprehend and continue.
- Dwell in love, serenity, and joy.
- Do not speculate on future events.
- Do not premeditate or anticipate.
- Live on the razor's edge, nothing ahead, nothing behind.
- Cease to hate.
- Cease to make choices.
- Cease to cling to opinions.
- Cease to seek the Truth.
- Cease mental agitation.
- Cease to do violence.
- Cease avid desiring.
- Cease to fear.

23

ODDS, ENDS, AND OPINIONS

Comment on a collection of subjects is included here with the intention of helping beginning meditators. Opinion is offered tentatively. There is no requirement that the reader accept as a matter of fact what is presented.

On Gurus—

Everyone wants a teacher, especially beginners, and it is indeed a wonderful experience when student and teacher meet. Some sects, particularly yogic, aver that spiritual progress is possible only under the guidance of a Guru and direct us to find one at once. Elsewhere we read that when the time is right the teacher will appear. Don't worry about it. It is the one problem that will take care of itself. Teacher and student will meet when they must and neither the student or the teacher will have any choice in the matter. Meeting your teacher is not going to solve your problem but only intensify it. There is much a teacher can do for you. But the more he does for you the more you must do for yourself. There is no use having a teacher if you don't do what he says but very often you can't do it no matter how hard you try. Try to understand that failure is also progress.

Responsibility—

Buddha placed the responsibility for enlightenment directly on the shoulders of the individual and challenged him to do his own religious seeking. *"Do not accept what ye hear by report. Do not accept tradition. Do not accept what is found books, nor because it is in accord with your beliefs, nor because it is the saying of your teacher. Be ye lamps unto yourselves. Those who after I am dead rely on themselves only and not look for assistance from anyone else, it is they who will reach the topmost heights."* That is **not** to say no schools, no teachers, no brotherhoods but does say unequivocably **no dependence.**

Meditation Techniques

We must be careful not to excitedly search for meditation techniques just in order to practice them or to accept them just because they are promoted by a successful teacher. What is helpful is to have a meditation plan or system of meditation beginning with a simple practice continuing through increasing difficulty with the possibility of enlightenment at the end. From the beginning is it helpful is we understand how our system works and what we can expect from it as we proceed from day to day. Thus we have faith in the method we use and feel assured that when the time comes we will have learned enough so that we can work with our teacher.

Desire

We hear that desire is the problem of life and is the basis for our inability to see directly, life as it really is. The mind is a sensuous organ and keeps one desire or another before us continually in order to achieve satisfaction. If you don't believe it, watch the mind after the loss of a

Odds, Ends and Opinions

loved one. We are advised to cease desiring and indeed we must before we can realize. But what of the desire for enlightenment. Is that not the volition, the motivating force, the speechless necessity that drives us to Reality? Let it be the last to go, for without it life is empty. But is not emptiness our goal?

Determination

Our practice of meditation must become the main thrust of our existence, the conscious meaning in our lives and all other activities ultimately must become subordinate to it. It must become the test bed for our experience. We must trust ourselves and see that what works in meditation is what is true. If chanting, postures, prayer, ritual, friendship and love support our practice in daily life, use them. When they do not support, reject them. A certain toughness of mind, even ruthlessness may sometimes be necessary.

Over the doorways of some Zen Temples is written, *"Zen is a matter of life and death"* or *"Those not concerned with life and death, do not enter here."*

Concepts

Metaphysical concepts are useful in as much as they contribute to functional daily activity. Conceptual speculations can become ties, irrelevent to the hard practical work of releasing the human spirit. Avoid speculation. It is profitless. Whether the world is finite or infinite whether soul and the body are the same or different, whether the soul exists after death or not the Buddha did not explain. The practical program of concentration and meditation in life leaves no time for profitless speculation.

Balance

Those who persevere in meditation are not those who blindly practice according to teachers' directions. Nor are they those who only study the theory of meditation and the elements of oriental philosophy. Balance is needed, both practice and understanding. Enough philosophy must be assimilated, later to be confirmed in meditation, so that a trust in the system arises. There is indeed a psychological turnover, distinctly noticeable in the aspirant. A certainty develops that the path is indeed his own.

Paths

There is no Yogic path, no Bhakti, no Karma, no Raja, no Kriya Yoga. There is no path of the Sufi, no Noble Eightfold Path. Only your path exists. Any conceptual way to God or Reality is OK if you think it is. No one way is better or worse than another. Stay relaxed. Take advantage of every spiritual opportunity, try any path that presents itself. Continue to trust yourself. Change paths at the drop of a hat if so inspired. Look around. When your path crystalizes and you know what to do, do it.

Practice

Regular practice is the key to progress as it is in any physical or mental effort. Take a tip from the athlete and see how he trains. He runs ten miles daily. He dribbles a basketball eight hours a day. He trains the body. You train the mind. Repetition is important.

Progress

Progress in meditation cannot be determined by the beginner and can only generally be seen by the experienced meditator. Every sitting is progress. Every effort is helpful. When we think we have had a *"good"* meditation because the mind has held steady on the object, is that really as *"good"* as when we have had to laboriously return the distracted mind again and again to the object? Continue, nothing but progress is possible.

Friends

Friends are helpful and necessary. To succeed, do things together. A close relationship develops among meditators and a constructive atmosphere is sensed directly. The meditation room has a feeling all of its own.

Purity

It is not necessary to be sinful or sinless, clean or unclean, pure or impure in order to meditate—unless it interferes. Relinquishment is a continuing process throughout the evolution of one's meditation. What can be accommodated at one point becomes intolerable at another. A good rule is this; if the activity interferes with meditation, change it. If overeating, excessive sexual activity, smoking or hatred interfere, they must go.

Food

People who do not eat meat or eat very little and consume mostly vegetables seem to remain slender and to have more energy than others.

Smoking

Smoking tends to deplete energy in the body which is just what one would expect. Once one becomes accustomed to the higher level of energy and has some skill in its management smoking becomes an undesirable habit. If one smokes heavily, he may not be able to experience the flow of energy at all.

Books

A book list is included here. The books provide and emphasize a necessary introduction to oriental thought and feature various methods of meditation.

Book List—
- Religions of Man—*Huston Smith*
- The Secret Path—*Paul Brunton*
- The Book—*Alan Watts*
- A Primer of Soto Zen—*Dogen-Masunaga*
- Zen Flesh, Zen Bones—*Paul Reps*
- The Practice of Zen—*Garma CC Chang*
- The Zen Teaching of Huang Po—*John Blofeld*
- Ask The Awakened—*Wei Wu Wei*
- Secret of the Lotus—*Donald Swearer*
- Real Way to Awakening—*Dhammasudhi*
- Heart of Buddhist Meditation—*Thera*
- The Power of Mindfulness—*Nyaniponika Thera*
- Practical Insight Meditation—*Sayadaw*
- Secrets of Chinese Meditation—*Charles Luk*
- Tibets Great Yogi Milarepa—*Evans Wentz*
- Teachings of the Compassionate Buddha—*E.A. Burtt*
- I Am The Gate—*Bhagwan Shiree Rajneesh*
- Fundamentals of Yoga—*Rammurti Mishra*

Odds, Ends and Opinions

Taoist Yoga—*Lu K'uan Yu*
The Mysterious Kundalini—*Vasant G. Rele*
Practical Lessons in Yoga—*Swami Sivananda*
Practical Mysticism—*Underhill*
Vedanta For The Western World—*Isherwood*

Hopefully we may somehow see for just a moment that we are not what we think we are, that we really are not the categories we conceptualize ourselves to be. A Christian, a Buddhist, a Moslem is not possible except conceptually and we need not be enlightened to see this—only for a moment without opinion. It is hardly possible to be separate from the universe as humans but lets pretend that we are in fact separate. If so then we are entitled to the best and the worst of the history and knowledge of **all** religions of man simply because we are human. Furthermore it is not necessary that we **belong** to any of them. We can use them at will. We can change at will in order to find our path to Reality.

It is most important to realize that we must see for ourselves. Teachers do but point the way, and inevitably the direction they point is inward. Meditation is an inward art and an inner way. Meditation is learning to see directly. The practice is not Eastern, Western, Buddhist or Christian, it simply is! And it is sorely needed by those of us who seek Unity.

In closing a few quotations are appropriate:

- As long as there is a "you" doing or not-doing anything, "meditating" or "not-meditating," "you" are no nearer home than the day you were "born." However many years you may have been at it, and whatever you have understood or have not understood, you have not yet started if there is still a "you" in the saddle. As long as you do anything as from a "you," you are in bondage.—*Wei Wu Wei*

- The greatest man of all is nobody.—*Traditional*
- There is nothing so far removed from us as to be beyond our reach or so hidden that we cannot discover it.—*Descartes*

If meditation appeals to you, I urge you to begin and with all my heart, I wish you success in the endeavor.

In Metta, (Lovingkindness)

Bob Maitland

About The Author

Robert Maitland was born in Coatesville, Pennsylvania, a small city thirty miles west of Philadelphia, in 1922. The city is an agricultural center whose economy is largely dependent upon the steel industry. He was the son of a house painter and crane operator.

He graduated from high school in 1940 and worked as a gandy dancer on the Pennsylvania Railroad and as a welder in a steel company. He enlisted in the USNR as a Naval Aviation Cadet in January of 1943 and graduated as a Naval Aviator 20 months later. He served for a year in the Pacific area as a carrier based, fighter pilot during the remainder of World War II.

In Semptember of 1948 he married Marguerite Casey and they now have three daughters.

Subsequently, under the GI Bill, he graduated from Penn State University, degreed as a B.S. in Physics and as an Electrical Engineer from the University of Miami, Florida.

He has worked for the General Electric Company for 22 years both in engineering and management. He has been associated with the Apollo Program working in support of the NASA Marshall Space Flight Center for 11 years.

In the mid-fifties he became interested in Oriental Religions and Philosophies and explored the existing literature until the late sixties. His prevailing interest however was the practice of meditation and much effort was given to attempt to meditate from book instructions.

In 1970 he formalized what he had learned and upon request began classes in meditation in Huntsville, Alabama at the Free University of Alabama and at the local Unitarian Church which are still continuing.

In February 1972, he wrote to the Hui Neng Zen Temple at Easton, Pa. requesting admission for Zen training. The response from Abbot Hearn was positive, sympathetic and encouraging. Continued correspondence followed and shortly thereafter Master Hearn visited Huntsville where he lectured on "Origins of Zen" and "Training of the Zen Monk." Mr. Maitland visited Hui Neng Temple for a week's meditation training during middle August. At the end of August under the sponsorship of Master Song Ryong Hearn, Mr. Maitland was ordained in absentia, Upasaka (lay disciple), Tae Chi, to master Il-Bung Seo. During the course of the next year, a group of meditators formed in Huntsville. Eight of them visited Hui Neng Zen Temple along with Mr. Maitland in August of 1973 where they received Buddhist names and meditation training from the Venerable Korean Zen Master Il-Bung Seo, Kyung Bo. Upon return to Huntsville, the nine formed the nucleus of a meditation group "the Friends Meditation Club" sponsored by Master Seo, which continued to grow. Disciple Maitland was called to San Francisco, California during August 1974 where he was ordained a Dharma Master (lay Zen Minister) and authorized to start a Zen center in Huntsville with the understanding that Master Seo would come to the USA from Korea for permanent residence and that support would be received from Master Seo's descendent Masters Song Ryong Hearn and Tae Hui Gilbert. In San Francisco, a Holy Name ceremony was held by Master Seo and eight more Huntsville students were named in absentia. Upon his return, Maitland proposed the formation of a Zen Center in Huntsville in the line of Dharma Father Seo. From the monthly donations of students and friends, a house at 307 8th Street, Huntsville, Ala., was rented in October of 1974 and the Il-Bung Zen Center was founded.

Zen Master Song Ryong Hearn, English born, the grand nephew of the famous interpreter of Japan Lafcadio Hearn, is a Dharma successor of Master Il Bung Seo, Kying Bon and is presently travelling in Asia.

Zen Master Tae Hui Gilbert, American born, is a Dharma Successor of Master Il Bung Seo, Kyung Bo and is currently the Master in Residence of the Il Bung Son Won at 2080 Green St., San Francisco, CA.